Making a Fortune

Making a Fortune

Learning from the Asian Phenomenon

Spinder Dhaliwal

CAPSTONE
be inspired!

John Wiley & Sons, Ltd

Other Wiley Editorial Offices

I dedicate this book to my Mum and Dad

Contents

Acknowledgements

When I decided to write this I thought, I am just going to see what happens, I am going to let God and the Universe guide me. I could not have found more serendipitous circumstances. I met the dynamic Emma Swaisland who, in her wisdom, commissioned the book. Contacting the entrepreneurs and getting them on side was amazing; they could not have done more. Their personnel were incredible and eased my access to all quarters. I also got my family and friends, in particular Andy Adcroft, John Wheeler and Bal Basra, to help proof-read the chapters which they did with such generosity. I thank all at *Eastern Eye* who commissioned me to compile *Britain's Richest Asians* in *Success* magazine which built on the earlier success of my Centre for Asian Entrepreneurial Research. I am grateful to them all.

This is a book which belongs to the Asian community and is a dedication to its hard work and spirit and what it has brought to the UK. I could not have done this without the work and strength and courage of the first generation, who left so much emotionally back 'home', and the second generation who had many challenges to deal with, respecting the values of the first generation whilst trying to integrate and get on in a new society. A lot of tears have been shed in the process and a lot of hearts broken, wondering if the price was worth it. I hope this book serves as an inspiration to show that it was.

I thank Anthony Haynes, Jenny Ng, Jasmine Basra, Elizabeth Allen, Shalin Punn, Wendy Jackson, Ben Egan, Kara Jenkins, Melanie Hadaway, Mary McGowan, Rachel Clarke, Collette Smith, Brian McEwan, Shirley Anderson, Sarteca Madan, Hannah Smith, Chantal Hill and, of course, my 'dream team' of entrepreneurs.

'Finally I would like to thank the following for kindly allowing me to use their logos on the front cover: Arora Holdings Limited, Nat Puri, Gulam Noon, Firoz Kassam, Shami Ahmed, Robert Davis (ebookers .com), Kartar Lalvani, Perween Warsi, Dynshaw Italia (Cobra) and Waymade Healthcare PLC.'

Forewords

The Businessman

The world of enterprise is one of great excitement, constant challenges and unlimited opportunities. There's no set formula to becoming an entrepreneur; you can't create a mathematical solution that you simply follow. It's all about people with spirit, relentless passion and an overwhelming determination to succeed no matter what obstacles they face along the way.

One of the great attributes of many entrepreneurs is their passion to inspire others, to educate by sharing their own learnings and experiences in order to keep the entrepreneurial spirit alive and encourage the current and next generation to follow their dream. These biographies bring this spirit to life and give you an unprecedented insight into these individuals' lives as they share with you their triumphs, their mistakes and their personal and professional development.

What makes a business successful is the people. Get the right people in the right place and an organization will work far more efficiently and effectively. Across the profiles there is a wide selection of businesses covered, whether they are product focused or service driven. But while each business may be different and each person has their own story to tell, what you can be sure of is that it's their characteristics that will come through as driving their progression and their ultimate success.

As these biographies delve into the lives of these highly successful businessmen and women you can travel through their personal and professional journeys and learn from the analysis of how they deal with their fair share of challenges. Understand how each individual has turned their dream into a reality, discover how they learnt from mistakes, picked themselves up after facing challenges, embraced growth and made decisions – difficult or otherwise – all of which will have contributed to who they are today.

More importantly you'll have insight into their story from the outset, uncovering their childhood and their personal lives. From challenging upbringings to enjoying strong foundations for the future, these initial years still play a key role in each person's profile. Even the most challenging of personal experiences, taking tragic or drastic turns, can only enrich the entrepreneurial spirit. Being an entrepreneur is more than just a full-time job; it's your life, so it's important to see all the pieces of this jigsaw together.

Asian or not, you will take something away with you that will give you a greater insight into one of the most exciting and rewarding aspects of today's business world.

Enjoy the ride with these businessmen and women as being an entrepreneur is as much about the journey as it is about the end success.

Mike Jatania

Chief Executive, Lornamead Group

The Academic

This is an important book. This book matters. This is not a work like Tarantino's *Pulp Fiction* where there is a plot but no real characters. There is a story behind this book, for sure, which is made up of many plots and the plots have enough to keep most people interested. There are plots with twists and turns, there is success, there is failure, rags to riches, conservatism and unconventionality, bricks and mortar, clicks and free kicks. If the book isn't like *Pulp Fiction* then it's also not like *Seinfeld*, where there are characters but no plots. Every one of these plots gives us the profile of a real person, a well-rounded character, with all the traits that real people have. Some are driven, some more laid back. Some work through conviction and others through consensus. Some we will want to know better, others we will maybe know too much about. All of them are achievers, all of them are interesting, all of them have a story worth reading. This mixture of plots and characters makes the book good but doesn't necessarily make it important. This book matters for other reasons.

In this age of non-judgement, many things are no longer seen as being better or worse, important or unimportant, good or bad. Now things are simply different; one view of the world, be it cultural, social, economic or political, has as much merit as any other view of the world. Opinions are not differentiated on the basis of their foundation or merit, their theory or evidence, and everyone must have a say whether it is on the daytime television chat shows, the radio phone-in vox pops or the internet's blogosphere. But, for most of us anyway, some things are better than other things. Some things do matter more than other things. Occasionally, the world is absolute and things are black or white and not grey. This book has value for many reasons which go beyond the intrinsic value that all books have in and of themselves. This book matters because of its timing as well as its content and for the story behind it as much as the stories within it.

This book appears at just the right time. The historian Amy Henderson frequently discusses the role of heroes in society. For time immemorial, societies have looked to their heroes as role models and exemplars, from the generals in Ancient Rome and the monarchs of the Middle Ages through to the pioneers who tamed the Wild West. Society not only looks up to its heroes but those heroes are a reflection of the norms and values held by that society. So who are the heroes and role models of today's society? In this post-modern world, heroes increasingly become anyone who is famous regardless of where that fame comes from. Famous as an inventor? A scientist? Famous for politics or for philanthropy? Society increasingly fails to differentiate and so, from the winners and losers of reality television shows through to anyone with a mouse and internet connection, all can have their 25 minutes in the spotlight. Heroes and role models shouldn't be like this. If we are to look up to people we should do it for better reasons than just because they appear on TV or the front cover of glossy magazines. The dictionary tells us that heroes are people who are admired for their deeds, for what they do and what they achieve. Heroes have a legacy. They have substance. This book is important because it provides some modern economic heroes of real substance and a collection of role models with real achievements behind them.

In some of her more academic work, Spinder Dhaliwal talks about how there is always some element of 'geographic chronology' to the successful entrepreneur: being in, and recognizing that you are in, the right place at the right time really matters. We live in uneasy times. Globalization has changed the economic world of certainty into a world of insecurity where the ever freer movement of goods, capital and labour has changed all of our economic landscapes and prospects. The contracting out of services to Indian call centres, the shift of manufacturing jobs to China and the arrival on our shores of economic migrants has created an atmosphere of unease and maybe even hostility. This book should be an antidote to all that. In the middle of an overemotional and frequently ill-informed debate, where a Prime Minister can talk, using someone else's language, about 'British jobs for British people', this book shows the real contribution of these economic actors. First, second and third generation Asian entrepreneurs, in the main quietly and without a fuss, have made their fortunes and created wealth and opportunity in the UK that, without them, would never have existed. How have they done it? Sure there are all the unique characteristics of the entrepreneur, seeing things that no one else sees, but there is also hard work, thrift, modesty, playing by the rules. This book tells Asian stories but it is also a very British tale, or at least we'd like to think so.

So what are these stories? Whilst this is an anthology of Asian success stories, the author's tale is as much a part of it as anything. This book represents the culmination of Spinder Dhaliwal's professional and personal journey through Asian entrepreneurship and success. Spinder's story begins in the stereotypical Asian corner shop with the expected long hours, hard work and family commitment. Like many of her generation, Spinder found a new route through education, but where Spinder's story takes a different track is in the use of her education to champion and chronicle her community and not escape from it. From the founding and directing of the Centre for Asian Entrepreneurial Research in the mid-1990s through to the five years spent editing the annual *Asian Rich List*, her life has become interlinked and intertwined with the people in this book. The combination of experience and research, theory and practice, networks and independence means that there is no one better qualified to write about these important issues.

Let's place it in a wider context. Spinder's empirical research shows that the Asian wealth-creating sector in the UK creates wealth in high-value, high-tech and high-skilled sectors like pharmaceuticals, fashion and IT. Surprised? You probably should be. Maybe Asian entrepreneurs have spent too long not causing a fuss, maybe they are too modest, too British even. This is a book which tells many of the stories behind these numbers, and if the entrepreneurs won't cause a fuss then it's probably a good job that Spinder Dhaliwal has, because every success needs an advocate, every good story should be told.

Plots. Characters. Heroes. Substance. This is a good book. And an important one.

Dr Andy Adcroft FRSA

Introduction

'The real measure of success comes, not during times of comfort and convenience, but at times of challenge and controversy,' wrote Martin Luther King. The world has indeed become more challenging and also more controversial. In the past few decades when the economy has teetered on the brink of recession, propped up by short-term consumer spending and rising house prices, where stock market values, not only in the UK but at a global level, have declined sharply and where faith and trust in institutions and role models has been significantly diminished, this book offers what Gandhi referred to as 'optimism on solid facts'.

For two decades, entrepreneurs have been eulogised in the popular press. At a time when real heroes are hard to find, it is the entrepreneur, the dynamic go-getting risk taker, who has become the hero of free enterprise. At the cutting edge of the British entrepreneurial community are the Asian businesses featured in this book. It is a fascinating tale. It takes in businesses from manufacturing to finance, from food to hotels, from pharmaceuticals to fashion. It includes first-, second- and third-generation achievers. It provides the definitive guide to 'who's who' in the Asian business world.

At the end of *The Producers*, Mel Brooks asks 'where did we go right?'. I asked myself the same question at the start of this book. If the results of these entrepreneurs were achieved in decades full of challenge and controversy, the past few years have been no different: sluggish economic growth, stock market uncertainty and question marks about the housing market provide the starkest of economic backdrops to this compendium of Asian success.

Through case studies and analysis of both personal and business issues, I illustrate the triumphs and challenges facing these individuals, how disasters were overcome and how they fought against the odds to be outstanding role models for anyone interested in business or making money. I tell a story of grit and determination to succeed, and draw out the lessons so anyone, whether budding or existing entrepreneurs, Asian or not, can learn from these amazing individuals.

If nothing else, this book is testament to the diversity of Asian talent in the UK. As well as diversity there is also change. Perhaps the era of the privately owned Asian business is coming to an end. These businesses have raised millions in new capital despite the harshest of climates.

Their success testifies to the staying power of Asian business which successfully combines the dynamism of the free market with the go-getting, risk-taking heroism of the entrepreneur. Not forgetting, of course, the values of family, thrift and hard work and a commitment to the community. This book celebrates both doing good by doing well and doing well by doing good.

Cynic and wit Cyril Connolly noted that 'whom the gods wish to destroy they first call promising'. In this world he could not have been more wrong. If the past is a guide to the future, then these entrepreneurial stars will be household names in years to come. As Asian wealth spreads outwards and upwards we have more and more facts in which to ground our optimism.

As I said earlier, Asian wealth has grown and become more diverse. It now crosses from first through second and third generations. It spans manufacturing and services, entertainment and fashion, hotels and property, food and pharmaceuticals. Would we like more tycoons? Absolutely. We all recognize their contribution, so would we like more women entrepreneurs? Without a doubt. Maybe we should just give it a little more time because, if success is a science, this is one community where the conditions are met and the result is bound to happen. That's confidence, not complacency.

Money is better than poverty, but not only for financial reasons. Asian wealth represents solid foundations, good business practice, commitment to community, openness to change and a massive contribution to society.

This book can show you the money. Asian wealth creators have created wealth faster than the rest of the economy. They have bucked the trend this year as they did last year and the year before that. Asian wealth now creates and sustains more jobs than it has ever done. Asian wealth stimulates growth in industries and places that would struggle without the engine of Asian entrepreneurship. Asian wealth is diversifying. Asian wealth is modernizing. Asian wealth crosses the generational divide. If you want new and old economy wealth, it's in these pages. If you want modern and traditional management practices, they are in this book. If you want a new generation of entrepreneurs and wealth creators, read on.

Jerry Maguire would hate this. Celebrating wealth for the sake of wealth could easily be described as shallow. Perhaps money is like manure, where its value only becomes apparent when it is spread around so that other things can grow. So again, what have I learnt? Something more than just numbers? I have learnt some fascinating stories from fascinating people. Some of them are tales of rags to riches but many of them go much deeper. I have learnt about the complexities of communities that, at some levels, are fully incorporated into their host societies and that, at others, remain separate. I have learnt that both prejudice and pride plays a part in these success stories. I have learnt that these are real financial and non-financial triumphs and that we shouldn't be slow or quiet or reticent about telling the world. And celebrating them.

Liberty Island in the United States got its monument 120 years ago. The statue came with a promise of a haven for the tired, poor and huddled masses who wanted to seize the opportunity of the American Dream. There is no similar monument (or perhaps sentiment) to be found at the port of Dover or the airports of London. I'm not sure if those who made it into this book were ever tired, poor or huddled but they, their parents or their grandparents certainly came. This book celebrates them and their achievement. Maybe, and more importantly, this book celebrates their contribution to their own and other communities. This book will show you the money but, I hope, it will show you much, much more.

For half a decade now, spring has meant research and deadlines. For the past five years I have compiled the flagship publication 'Britain's Richest Asians' in *Success* magazine, which is an annual supplement for *Eastern Eye* newspaper. It has meant last-minute panics about facts and figures. When I started doing this, spring was just about the numbers before it became about stories too. But it always came with pressure.

The outcome of all this I love. We should celebrate the achievements in our communities, we should recognise the talents that make those achievements possible, we should be more confident and proud about what we do. After five years of this, it's a good time to sit back and think. Not about what I've learnt but about why I do it – again and again and again. What is about these people that makes their stories so compelling? Why do I always want to come back to chronicle the next episode in the drama that is Asian wealth creation? Perhaps it's the familiarity. Like any good drama, it has a strong list of characters that I've come to know, to feel comfortable with and to understand. I just tell the stories, it's the creators and entrepreneurs who make them.

But wait, don't they say that familiarity breeds contempt? There must be more to doing this than telling the same story year after year. There is. A good drama needs a plot, things have to happen; as well as continuity there must also be change. When I started doing this, Asian wealth was Asian wealth and threw up few surprises. Sure, there was a lot of it (now there's even more) and it was where you would expect to find it. Asian wealth was in manufacturing, retailing and textiles. Now Asian wealth, as well as being traditional, is also new. The plot has thickened and moved into IT, pharmaceuticals, fashion and the media.

By profession, I'm an academic. Day to day, in my teaching and in my research, I deal with the relationship between theory and practice. But, most of the time, I deal with the theory. How things could be. How things should be. How things may be. I think that's why I've kept doing this. It gives me a break from theory. When spring appears, I get to deal with how things are. And things are pretty good. With every episode, they've got better. This has been a great drama to write.

There are still some things missing from this book. There are just a few women but we should never forget the pivotal roles played in these businesses by our so-called 'silent contributors'. The book is testament to men and women of vision, dynamism and acumen. It is, no doubt, a book built on the principles of family, thrift and hard work but it is also a book of people who are not afraid to embrace change, who create the wealth on which the economy is built and who make major contributions to the society in which they have prospered. At a time when role models have been hard to come by, we have found some.

Spinder Dhaliwal

Shami Ahmed and Family

Reproduced by permission of Shami Ahmed

As both a brand and an individual, Shami Ahmed has crossed over into mainstream British life. If you follow fashion and want to look good, odds are that somewhere in your wardrobe is the Legendary Joe Bloggs label. Under the name Juice Corporation, the business has grown from the core Joe Bloggs brand to include designer brands such as Katharine Hamnett and Elizabeth Emanuel. Rarely out of the news, Shami Ahmed's eclectic mix of businesses, from fashion to property to finance, continues to work as well as ever. And all this from a man who started out as a market trader in

Burnley. His brand label now sells worldwide. Joe Bloggs has transcended the 80s and 90s, entering the new millennium with a fresh direction. Shami has faced challenges and hardships both professionally and personally in his rise to the top. Already worth an estimated £120 million, this is a family proud of its successes, its rebellions and its style.

Chapter 1

An Entrepreneurial Family

Born in Karachi, Pakistan on December 7, 1962, Shami Ahmed is now the Managing Director of the Juice Corporation which includes a premium portfolio of designer brands such as Joe Bloggs, Elizabeth Emanuel, Katherine Hamnett, Loyalty and Faith and Slazenger amongst others. The global success the company enjoys is attributed to the foundations laid by Shami's parents, the late Nizam Ahmed and his wife Saeeda. If growing up in an entrepreneurial environment plants the seeds of success for later life, then the little Ahmeds were in luck as all five children – Shami being the eldest son – have been actively involved in the business from the moment they could walk.

The Ahmed family settled in the north of England, in Burnley, when Shami was 2 years old. The start of what was to become a fashion empire was modest. In 1966, Shami's father set up a market stall selling socks and ladies' stockings. Hard work is the backbone of almost every Asian entrepreneurial success story and the Ahmeds are no different. Nizam and Saeeda juggled the responsibilities of raising a young family with working long hours in a strenuous business; all the children were encouraged to help out. There is no substitute for hard work and the Ahmed children had to shoulder responsibility from an early age. Bushra Ahmed is the eldest daughter and as far back as she can remember she was helping with the business. At 6 years old, she recalls, 'I was packing tights in boxes so my father could sell them'. Her brother Shami remembers catching the bus after school in Burnley to go to Manchester so that he could help out on the stall. Fashion is a fun business, but also one which demands that you put in the hours.

The first generation of Asian immigrants in the UK tried to create a secure home environment where their traditions and values could be retained. There was great emphasis on the importance of the family unit and the wider community network. Children were bought up to respect their elders and the elders in turn would do anything to better the situation of the young. They were prepared to work long hours and make many sacrifices for a better future. Duty, obligation and trust are key words in any Asian household. The unusual feature in the Ahmed family is that they do not overly value formal education, preferring the hands-on approach instead. Whilst most Asian parents stress the need to study further, and make many sacrifices for their children to gain academic qualifications, the Ahmeds are firm believers in practical experience. The business always came first, education was not as important and this was the case for the boys as well as the girls. The lack of academic training has not held them back in any way. This is an example of an Asian success story where the first generation initiated the business and the second generation made the move from small-time enterprise to multimillion-pound empire. The children were keen to move the business forward and the parents were willing to take the risks to do this. This story illustrates that the success and effort of the first generation immigrants can be taken forward to the next level.

The Female Perspective – Bushra's Role

The comfortable lifestyle that Bushra is now so accustomed to was not in evidence during her early years when she attended Rose Hill Junior School and then Walsall High School for girls. These were both state schools and her contempt for academia is plainly revealed by her remark, 'I was crap at school and I don't care who knows it'. Like her brother Shami, she preferred practical experience to classroom learning. Since she was clearly not academically inclined she left school at the first available opportunity and joined the business full time, an easy transition for someone who had been involved in it practically from the day she could walk.

This was a strategically important event for the family as it gave her father the freedom to launch a new venture. He was considering moving into the wholesale business in Manchester, and could concentrate on this now that Bushra was involved on a full time basis. The move from retail into wholesale was instigated by the younger Ahmeds, Bushra and Shami, who were the real driving force behind it. The Ahmeds never shy away from the risk and challenge of new ventures and succeeded in setting up Pennywise Cash and Carry, which is still thriving today.

The development of the business from a couple of retail shops to a wholesale clothes cash and carry was a move in the right direction for young Shami. Like Bushra, Shami did not study beyond O levels, left school at 15 and joined the business full time. He had big dreams and was eager to work on his vision for the family business. By now, he had the reputation of being a sharp dresser and was known for his fashion statements. He loved working with his father; they were a dynamic team, an entrepreneurial family at its best. While Nizam and Shami developed their plans for wholesale, Shami's mother and sisters ran the retail stores. In 1980 Pennywise Cash and Carry was established, based in Bury New Road, Manchester where it still operates today under the name of The Juice Corporation.

Bushra credits her formative years of 'training', when she was given a lot of responsibility, as the basis of her success today. Those early days strengthened her and made her more streetwise as she had to prove her mettle. Despite her parents' belief in her abilities she still had to prove her credibility to others. Being Asian, female and Muslim was interesting and, on top of that, she was still only 15 years old when she was given the job of making purchases for the retail shops. Trying to negotiate and haggle, she had to overcome the patronising attitudes of men who only wanted to deal with her father. Today respect is automatic, given the phenomenal success of their businesses. Bushra is now the leading lady of the company, thrives on the fast pace of the industry and loves making decisions, wheeling and dealing and being involved in every aspect of the fashion business. She is strong-minded, sharp and impulsive, and once went into a shop to buy a T-shirt and emerged with a Harley Davidson! Her philosophy is to see your goals and then go for them, doing what it takes to achieve them. Bushra is the PR and Marketing Director of The Legendary Joe Bloggs company.

Nizam Ahmed passed away and his death was particularly devastating to Bushra, who felt acutely the devastating loss of a man who had been a tower of strength and source of advice all her life. The shock of the loss left the whole family so shattered that they feared they were incapable of carrying on without him. Nizam, however, had left a legacy of strength and unity which paid dividends. The Ahmeds are ultimately survivors and managed to endure the desolation of the following months to rebuild a stronger and more powerful empire. Bushra describes her father as the most honest man she has known: 'He was very strong willed but fair', she reminisces. He gave his children much liberty and in return gained their utmost respect. His wife Saeeda played a pivotal role in the family. Saeeda, the 'silent contributor', is credited with originating the business and despite her modest profile is a shrewd businesswoman. Like many Asian women she is pivotal to the success of the business, and yet remains in the background. According to Bushra, 'my mother is generous, sensitive to plight, charitable, honest and direct' – clearly directness is a characteristic that has been inherited by her children.

Shami – Young and Restless

Shami shrewdly managed to balance the conflicts of his youthful desire to break out and launch his own label with the Asian values of family unity and strength. Not content with the growing business, Shami felt it had plenty of scope to grow further and he wanted to create something he could associate with. He was young, good looking and very restless; he had worked now for many years in the business and was confident. He craved the glamour of the fashion world, on his terms. Frustrated with dealing with other designer labels, he longed for his own. He was keen to promote his own identity, but stay under the umbrella of the family and remain the dutiful son. In 1986, the 24-year-old Shami created his Legendary Joe Bloggs label and it was exhilarating. He could not have known at the time that he had hit a formula for a global brand. It was his first taste of real success; he was marketing his own-brand label instead of other designers. He was ahead of the game, with his insider knowledge of the trade. Shami had identified a gap in the British market between expensive designer labels and cheaper, mass-produced jeans that anyone could wear.

His timing was perfect. The label was launched on the crest of the Manchester rave scene and even today the marketing team at Bloggs continues to watch movements on the street and in the music industry for inspiration. In the 1980s the designer jeans industry was geared for the elite but Shami felt that everyone should have the right to wear designer jeans. He saw a gap in the market for these jeans at low prices, enabling anyone and everyone to enjoy their glamour. He wanted to provide exciting garments with style, choice and, most of all, at a reasonable price.

Joe Bloggs took full advantage of the technology available, offering a wide range of washes on jeans. Shami produced a product for the mass market which is highly individual, and Joe Bloggs is one of the top ten bestselling brands of jeans in the UK today.

The Joe Bloggs operation required all of Shami's resources as he was now in the major league, dealing with designers, models and PR companies. The design team comprises both full-time staff and a network of freelance designers throughout Europe. There are also a number of graphic designers who develop designs for T-shirt motifs, swing tickets and garment labels. Extensive worldwide travel is undertaken to research new and innovative fabrics and trims as well as to buy materials.

The operation is not simple but Shami and family ensure that it is efficient. An example of this is the in-house export department which manages all overseas accounts and deals with international sale enquiries and new accounts. They work closely with the marketing team to ensure that monthly bulletins on Joe Bloggs' activity in the UK are forwarded to distributors worldwide. Regular meetings are held with all the key teams such as design, purchasing, marketing and export for feedback and communication, essential to sustain and increase sales. Quality control measures are in place and tests for wearability, durability and comfort take place on an ongoing basis. Garments are washed, tried, tested and measured to ensure exact specifications have been met. Finally, warehousing and distribution are aided by a fully computerized order-processing system, resulting in efficiency and accuracy. The sheer scale of the operation is miles away from market stall the family once ran.

As you would expect from a company at the leading edge of fashion, Joe Bloggs is innovative and creative. The whole process from design to manufacture is extremely fast moving and Shami Ahmed has made full use of professional and technical expertise. Expansion has been swift and other ranges developed include Bloggs for youths and Junior Bloggs, as well as Baby Bloggs. They also market footwear, toiletries and music. Joe Bloggs started with just a couple of styles of jeans and T-shirts; now there are over 100 designs as well as a range of clothes. An estimated 2000 people rely on Joe Bloggs in some way for their livelihood. The products are marketed in the Middle East and Far East as well as in Europe, but the UK still remains the base of the business and its largest market. The designer clothes industry is a fast-moving, highly competitive one with a high failure rate. The high costs of setting up in the industry are a barrier to new entrants. In this sense the

Ahmeds had the advantage of having one foot in the retail industry; they had their own cash and carry operation and workforce.

Top of the Pops

Shami's marketing strategy was innovative and daring; in the early stages he worked on gut instinct, never engaging consultants or undertaking market research. He had good instincts and acted on these. His own background made him well aware of class snobbery and the frustrations and dreams of escaping from the working class. Most designer labels were elitist and far removed from the masses he wanted to sell to. He felt it was unwise to compete at that level. There was a niche in the market for the everyday jeans wearer: 'any old Joe Bloggs'. Shami was desperately ambitious and insightful, so seized this opening that the million-pound designer jean companies had left and made his own fortune. He had the ability to gauge the needs of the people in the street and give them what they wanted.

He has since departed from his classless concept and diversified into other ranges such as Katherine Hamnett and Slazenger. He also boasts an elite clientele of pop stars, sports personalities and other notables. The marketing team design and coordinate promotions to specifically meet the needs of individual stockists. They keep their profile high due to their links with pop groups like Take That, Bad Boys Inc, New Order, Apache Indian and Happy Mondays. They were also commissioned to produce the most expensive pair of jeans in the world for the pop star Prince, valued at more than £100,000. They are linked with some high profile sports personalities such as Brian Lara, who holds the record for the highest ever score by a batsman in first-class cricket. But it was their marketing campaign in 1993, entitled 'Everyone Snogs in Joe Bloggs', that catapulted them to success and resulted in 86 percent brand awareness of their jeans: they were now a household name, all be it a classy one. More recently, spoon-bender Uri Geller has joined forces with Joe Bloggs to launch a range of clothing with the potential to allow the wearer to fulfil their dreams. Every product will be touched by Uri Geller before it hits the shop floor. Interesting!

This marketing effort is clearly a success factor in their business. Shami claims, 'the biggest failure is that many Asians do not know how to market themselves.' This is changing now as the business community has become aware of the value of marketing as a tool for success and generating sales. The first generation were prone to name businesses after themselves or their children, meaning that the name of the business often bore no relation to the product or service and in many cases was also very long, so it did not hit the right note for their target customer. They did not have the customer in mind. This is clearly changing, and today Asian entrepreneurs are at the global forefront of the marketing world and have created international, well-known brands which are household names.

Shami has since diversified his portfolio of business assets into finance and property and strengthened his fashion empire. Married now with a young son, you'd expect him to lead a quieter life. You would be wrong. Shami is not one to stay out of the limelight. He promotes his company at every opportunity and, with Bushra, has got marketing down to a fine art. He also seems to have a habit of hitting the headlines on a regular basis.

Turbulent Times – Moss Brothers

Shami's rebellious streak keeps him newsworthy, or is it just mischief that drives him? If he feels he is right, he goes a long way to prove this, leaving no stone unturned. New to the city, Shami bought and sold stakes in many retail outlets including House of Fraser, Peacocks, Austin Reed, Selfridges and also a 3 percent stake in Moss Brothers, which he subsequently increased to 5 percent and then 10 percent. The Moss Brothers Group consists of Cecil Gee, Moss, the Savoy Tailors Guild and the dress hire business. Shami became their biggest single shareholder, having accumulated many of the available shares in the tightly-held stock. His predatory instinct took over and he made an approach to buy the company. This approach was refused and an acrimonious battle ensued where he managed to force several Board changes and have new management in place, which led to a surge in the share price. The city had some fraught months with speculation as to Shami's role in Moss Brothers and they watched him make over 200 percent profits – despite not being able to buy the company. He then sold his entire stock in 2004, leading to takeover speculation. Accused by many of being a disruptive influence, the serial investor walked away with an estimated £9 million in profits. He admits his inexperience in handling this situation and says he would deal with it differently now: 'It was my first attempt in the city, I didn't know what I was up against.'

A Marriage of Great Inconvenience – the Elizabeth Emanuel Saga

Shami went on to be involved in one of the most bizarre and headline-grabbing cases in business history. Somehow, this market trader from Burnley crossed paths with Elizabeth Emanuel, the haute couture designer of Princess Diana's wedding dress. Emanuel was feted in celebrity circles after designing 'the' wedding dress in 1981. She opened her own store – called Elizabeth Emanuel – in London's Brook Street a decade later. However, in 1997, she was in severe financial difficulties and turned to Shami Ahmed to get her out of trouble.

Emanuel agreed to sell her business and its goodwill, including a registered trade mark for an Elizabeth Emanuel logo, to one of Shami's companies. It was to be a match made in heaven: the elitist designer and the young, dynamic entrepreneur. Emanuel also became an employee of an Ahmed company. As it turned out, it was a marriage of great inconvenience and a sore point to this day. The arrangement lasted barely a month, with Emanuel walking out, never to return. The following year Shami's company filed a UK trade mark application for the name Elizabeth Emanuel.

Emanuel was distraught, according to the headlines at the time, and a court battle commenced where she tried to reclaim the rights to her name which Shami had bought in 1997. Emanuel argued that as a designer she should be entitled to use her own name and no third party should be able to do so. Her defence continued that the public would be confused and assume that the designs had been made with the personal involvement of Elizabeth Emanuel. Shami's argument was straightforward, as reported by Graeme Colquhoun:

> 'If she had not sold the registered trademark for 'Elizabeth Emanuel', she would not have this problem. By making her name and the name of her business synonymous with each other, and then selling the business, she had ceded control over how her name may be used. Shami argued, in effect, that Elizabeth Emanuel wants to have her cake and eat it, by selling it to him and then claiming that he isn't allowed to use it in any case.'

The case was a clear-cut victory for Shami. In October 2002 the Trade Mark Registry ruled against Emanuel.

Shami reflects on the episode: 'I bought the brand and unfortunately Elizabeth came with it, with her ego and lack of business sense.' He recalls, 'The whole saga was a nightmare.' Shami, the son of a first generation Asian migrant who grew up with the ethics of hard work, prudence, saving and investing for the future and putting everything into the business was horrified when Emanuel wanted first-class travel and champagne parties: 'We did not travel first class ourselves, so to give her that privilege when she had not produced anything was not right. We could not work together.' Things then went from bad to worse: 'she tried to sue me for the return of her name. It reached the European Court of Justice and she lost.'

Making a Fortune – Perspectives from Shami

Shami Ahmed's success came from his ability to gauge the language of the streets. His direct approach is based on a canny exploitation of street cool and his brand was endorsed by Take That and Prince Naseem.

No stranger to the limelight or controversy, Shami became one of the richest and most famous young Asian businessmen in Britain; people could not get enough of him. He epitomised the young, successful entrepreneur and went on to present a Channel 4 TV series called *Dosh* which was aimed at showing how to get rich whilst still young. Despite turning his back on formal education, he was awarded an Honorary Graduate Open University degree in 2002.

Joe Bloggs was the first British company to break into Britain's top ten selling jeans brands. The Bloggs brand was central to the 1980s Manchester youth culture. It kept pace with existing trends and created new fashions with stone washed, 25-inch flares, drainpipes and ventilation jeans being examples. Under the name Juice Corporation, the business has grown from the core Joe Bloggs brand to include designer licensed brands such as Katharine Hamnett and sports brand Head, to owning the brand name Elizabeth Emanuel and franchising Joe Bloggs stores all over the world. It remains firmly in family ownership.

Joe Bloggs has entered the new millennium with a fresh direction. For such a young company, Bloggs already has a phenomenal heritage having pioneered trends and discovered rising stars that became icons of the decade, and even the era.

In recent years, the fashion end of the business has consolidated and internationalized; the company now employs more than 2000 people across the world. More properties have been bought across London and investments in companies like Austin Reed and Woolworths have driven the finance and investment business. Having made his first million before his twenty-fifth birthday, Shami and his family do not rest on their laurels but continue to build a business that becomes more and more legendary as each year passes. The next step is to take the brands online and to grow that way. Joe Bloggs Stores are also due to open in Dubai, South Africa, India and across the Middle East.

As a boss, Shami projects leadership qualities but he is willing to listen to good ideas. He encourages young, enthusiastic, ambitious, streetwise people to work for him. His management style is very hands-on, and he is actively involved with the day-to-day decisions and closely involved in every stage of the process from design to marketing. He is willing to invest in his company in terms of technology and talent as he feels the more you put into a business the more you get out. He employs professionals and does not believe in cutting corners.'

Shami feels that he is learning all the time. He has made mistakes in the past and has learnt and developed from the experience. His philosophy is that, on balance, if your strengths outweigh your weaknesses then you are on the right road. Shami is a great risk taker; he refers to it as 'calculated gambling' and this is the hallmark of Joe Bloggs' success. The team is not afraid to take risks. Their campaigns are daring and adventurous and they try and promote a glamorous, asexual image.

Having made his mark in fashion Shami is now enthusiastic about his property portfolio. He has an eclectic mix of businesses under his belt and through family trusts. Property is his passion now and he has various properties in the UK and overseas – Dubai, Cyprus, Germany, Bulgaria. The fashion side of the business these days is left to the family, with Bushra heading up the sales and marketing and working on a new online route for selling their brands.

Turning Points

So what as kept him ahead of the game despite all the trials and tribulations? He says, 'I worked hard, I started young, and I understood the sector well.' He showed great courage in creating Joe Bloggs and touching a nerve in the fickle world of fashion. 'I have a passion for anything I do, and I do it wholeheartedly. I dedicate my life to making a success of anything I do.'

Shami has not had a smooth ride: 'I have ups and downs in each and every area of my life but I am resilient.' He explains, 'I have made money and I have lost money.' Throughout all this he has managed to stay focused and determined. 'Losing is part of the learning curve and its value should not be underestimated.' He advises that, 'It's important to keep going, not to think of it as losing. You learn more by your mistakes and you come back stronger.'

His parents were his greatest inspiration: 'I was lucky as I watched and learnt from my parents; they were excellent role models – hard-working, sensible, down to earth.' He also credits starting young: 'I also had the opportunity of getting into the business at the age of 15. This meant I was ahead of my peers.' His parents are his inspiration and so too is his young son and wife: 'I'm doing this for my son now.' Does baby Bloggs appreciate this? Does he realize what an empire his father has created for him? As he's still under 10 years old, probably not.

Starting up Joe Bloggs was a key turning point. Shami says, 'We were in the right place at the right time.' This is modest of him; his passion for the Manchester scene and the ability to spot the right opportunities at that time held him in good stead too.

The management values in the organization to date have been largely the Asian values of family unity and even after the death of the founder, Nizam, his wife has resided over the empire, commanding the same respect. The second generation has brought in many Western business practices and ideologies but has remained faithful to its roots. Shami is currently based in London and the future success of the company is now in the hands of his brother Kashif, who is the Managing Director, and his sisters Bushra, Tabasum and Tesneem.

Shami has made his mark in the mainstream market and he is still only in his forties. He claims that his success is due mainly to the responsibility he was given at an early age. He has had practical experience in a very competitive industry and was fortunate to be encouraged and supported by his family. He is a great believer in using one's full potential and dislikes being held back or seeing others held back from achieving results. Shami adheres to the traditional Asian values of unity, drive and hard work and credits these values for his phenomenal success. He is an example of a successful second-generation Asian entrepreneur, the charismatic owner of Joe Bloggs and beyond, who developed his father's garment business, taking it forward by developing a brand name and modernizing it. Still young, Shami has experienced a lot of success and a lot of setbacks. He has a controversial image and has challenged the status quo. Despite this, the family are a great example of an Asian success story in the UK where they have battled against the odds and used their acumen to create and sustain a global brand. They have done it through sheer hard work and shown true grit. Whatever else happens, we are sure to see Shami hit the headlines again in the future.

Background Reading

Colquhoun, G., Associate, McGrigor Donald, Licensing Executives Society, Britain and Ireland. *News Exchange*, Issue 89: February – March 2003.

Foley, S., 'Moss Bros faces new speculation as Ahmed sells stake,' *Independent*, July 26, 2004.

RGC Jenkins & Co, *UK Diary: What's in a name*, www.jenkins-ip.com/mym/autumn2004/item_17.htm. Autumn 2004.

Mgadzah, R., 'A Mellow Blend of East and West,' *Sunday Telegraph*, Sept 15, 1991.

Uri Geller: www.uri-geller.com/tshirts.htm

Vasagar, J., Kelso, P.; James-Gregory, S. and Dodd, V., 'Shami Ahmed, 39, Businessman,' *Guardian*, June 17, 2002.

Surinder Arora

Photo supplied by Surinder Arora

The charismatic Surinder Arora is one of the top hoteliers in the UK. This is a story which reads like an Alan Ayckbourn play: it mixes confusion and enlightenment with hard work and inspiration. Running beneath is a sub-plot of steely determination which makes sense only when viewed with the surprises in the main text.

After an interesting childhood, where he grew up thinking his aunt was his mother, and an early career juggling several jobs, Surinder opened the Arora International at Heathrow. It was the first hotel in the UK purpose-built for airline crew and was successful due to Surinder's persistence and determination in the face of setbacks. A sister hotel opened at Gatwick in 2002 and now his portfolio is nationwide. He even boasts Sir Cliff Richard as a partner in one of his ventures. Surinder owns 14 major hotels nationally, and this figure is set to rise. Valued at an estimated £220 million, this dynamo goes from strength to strength.

Chapter 2

Mixed Blessings

The A4 in west London is home to some of the country's most popular hotels. Conveniently located near Heathrow, the world's busiest airport, these hotels are often the first port of call for both aircrew and travellers. The Arora International, opposite the British Airways Compass Centre, is Surinder's first hotel and is where he is still based. His office-cum-boardroom in the penthouse is surpassed only by the magnificent views from his roof-top golf garden of the runway with planes landing and taking off.

Surinder Arora is a fit man in his forties. Congenial, approachable, yet very, very busy. Busy but always charming enough to offer his visitors masala tea, a must in traditional hospitality.

He's experienced a taste of life in an Indian extended family, quite literally. Adopted at birth, he has had an unusual upbringing. His natural mother gave him away to her younger sister who had no children of her own. He was a 'mistake', he laughs; his mother had thought her family was complete until he popped up ten years after his older brother. So he grew up believing his aunt was his mother, and vice-versa. His natural parents left India for the UK soon after and he lived with his aunt and uncle, though he thought they were his parents. A confusing start to this story.

Surinder was born and raised in the Punjab region in India. He grew up spoilt and pampered as an only child to his aunt, who loved him dearly. His natural parents stayed in touch and visited often but, unaware of the ties, he recalls wondering, 'Why does my aunt love me more than her other nephews and nieces?' It didn't occur to the young child that she was his natural mother.

Despite his privileged upbringing as the doted-on 'son' in a loving household, he was a misguided youth. He did not fulfil his potential in India and fell in with a bad crowd. He became a spoilt, rebellious teenager. 'I wasn't studying, I gambled and got up to no good,' he confesses. His biological mother noted this with dismay on one of her frequent visits to India and suggested to her younger sister that he should come to England. They would get him to study and 'knock some sense into him,' he explains ruefully. His 'mother' agreed.

Boy to Man

As a result, in 1972 at the age of 13, Surinder came to Southall, England to be united with his natural family. At that time Southall, which is in west London close to Heathrow airport, boasted a high Asian population who were mainly from the Punjab area of India. This is changing now as new immigrant groups arrive. It was here he was to discover his true birthright. When he eventually found out that his 'aunt' was his real mum, he recalls, 'it was a shock.' Later, after it had sunk in, he says, 'I felt blessed with having two sets of mums and dads who looked out for me'.

It was in England that his real growth and development began and he was able to learn the importance of hard work and effort. It had a sobering effect on him. No longer left to be a pampered, spoilt kid, he watched his parents struggle to make money. He saw them prepared to work at two jobs each, in menial roles. 'My mother was a cleaner in the evenings,' he explains, having gained an appreciation of the value of money. Surinder's mother was well networked in the community. The work ethic is strong in the Asian community and highly prized; laziness is frowned upon. The close-knit community meets regularly at family functions and temples and so any news travels fast. The wider family networks serve to provide a source of expectations of behaviour and, since the reputation of the family is so closely linked to the community, the community exerts a strong influence. In practical terms it affects everyday behaviour and comments such as 'you can't be a failure' and 'what will people say?' are familiar sentiments to most Asians.

This was a rude awakening for the young Surinder. Another stumbling block (which was later to be his saviour) was that his mother was a force to be reckoned with. She was strict with him and wanted him to do well. Despite being bright, he was struggling at school; studying in a new language presented a barrier. Having spoken Punjabi all his life, it was difficult for him to articulate in English, and starting school in the UK at the age of 13 was not easy. Consequently, he did not excel in his studies and was held back a year at school which added to his woes. He recalls approaching his mathematics teacher, a fellow Punjabi, for help. This teacher then explained things to him in Punjabi and Surinder soon picked them up.

But it was not just school that presented a challenge to the young lad. His mother was the pivotal driver in his life, but his relationship with her was testing. Not prepared to have an idle son, the family work ethic soon rubbed off on young Surinder when his mother encouraged him to earn a wage. For a modest woman, she was extremely resourceful and she used her community contacts to get him a job in a local market where he made just £1.50 a day. He resented her during his school years: 'She never lets me do anything,' he remembers telling his best friend at school. His friend replied, 'My mother is dead, at least you have one'. That was a turning point for him: 'It was at that moment I realised how precious she was.'

Leaving school after his O levels, Surinder initially wanted to be a policeman. 'I wanted the uniform and the power,' he grins. Instead he met a friend who persuaded him to be a pilot. He went to the London School of Flying and loved it. However, he still needed a job and these were scarce. His mother, once again, came to his rescue and got him an interview through her contacts at British Airways. He got through the interview process and became an office junior. He earned £31 a week and his flying lessons cost him £21 an hour: 'I couldn't even afford two a week,' he laments. Such is the passion of Asian parents and their sense of duty towards their children: his parents were prepared to do anything for him, even going so far as to say they would mortgage their house to pay for his lessons. They helped him out and were the wind beneath his wings.

Surinder made up for lost time and drove himself relentlessly. Lazy in his early days, he began to understand the value and importance of hard work and was not afraid of getting his hands dirty. By now he was working evenings at the Penta hotel (now the Renaissance), as well as his day job. 'I worked really, really hard. From 9 a.m. until 2 a.m. with both jobs', he recalls proudly. 'I wanted that pilot's licence.' That was his driver. Sadly, his dream was not to be.

Clipped Wings

By the time he had accumulated enough hours for a commercial licence, there was a surplus of pilots and British Airways announced the closure of their school in Hamble. It was not a good time. Surinder continued working some time at the Penta hotel from 1978 to 1982 and full time in British Airways. His life revolved around work.

It was a chance visit that was to change his destiny and thrust him into the big time. An Abbey Life financial advisor saw his mum and dad regularly but Surinder recalls, 'I used to sneak out, I didn't want to see him'. Surinder was too engrossed in his work to waste time chatting to his parents' friends. His mother told the advisor sarcastically, 'The only way you can catch Surinder is to offer him work'. And he was offered a job; the advisor had spotted his talent for hard work and sensed his ambition. However, in typical Asian style, instead of giving up any of his jobs Surinder took two weeks' leave from British Airways to attend a training course for Abbey. 'I didn't want to do the Abbey training, I thought I would go on holiday instead,' he says. 'Mum made me,' he adds, ruefully. 'She said, "you have nothing to lose".' Maybe nothing to lose but, as we shall see, everything to gain. She was to carve out her son's destiny.

The year 1982 was an eventful one for him; he joined Abbey Life in September as a sales associate and got married in October. He recalls going to the Abbey Christmas party with his wife. 'I'd only been with them for a few months so we were seated at a table at the back of the room. There were over 300 people there.' On the top table sat all the senior managers and also the top financial advisor of the year. 'I did a double take' recalls Surinder, 'It was my old Punjabi mathematics teacher!'

Surinder aspired, then and there, to be seated on the top table by the following year. He was, and was again for the next five years, too. 'I drove myself hard. I was determined,' he says. It was not easy, though: 'I always say life is about ups and downs, valleys and hills. In my second year at Abbey I was in a deep valley but I never gave up. If you're willing to push yourself up that hill you will always be a success.' This human dynamo was, at this time, working multiple jobs and had been promoted to sales manager with Abbey: 'I worked full time at BA doing shifts from 6.30 a.m. to 2.30 p.m., I then went to Abbey Life from 3 p.m. to 6 p.m., home for 15 minutes and then saw clients all evening until 11.30 p.m.' If he was ever home before 11 p.m. his wife knew something was wrong. She used to say to the kids, 'See that picture behind the front door of that man? If he knocks on the door, let him in, he's your father!'

He started dabbling in property at this time too. Property investment is big business in the Asian community and is highly prized because property is a tangible asset and represents security. Surinder, like many others who made their fortunes in the Asian community and beyond, saved his money and invested in properties. The price rises of the 80s and the buy-to-let boom are key factors in the Asian success story.

Surinder firmly believes that to succeed you need the support of the family. 'I am lucky with my wife and my parents. This is where Asians have an advantage. The close-knit family helps a great deal. The extended family can be a blessing.' Surinder is not one to give up easily; he is a shrewd salesman, he understood people and could turn a 'no' into a 'yes' – perfect training for the challenges he was to face in the hospitality industry.

Arora Takes Off

Gaps are all around us, in everything we do and all that we see. There are those small gaps in our day-to-day lives when we wish someone would invent that gadget to make our lives just a fraction easier or better. There are gaps in our professional lives. Things we do ourselves that we wish we could pay someone else to do. We are told that nature abhors a vacuum, that as soon as a gap appears someone or something fills it. What marks Surinder Arora out as different is just this – he sees gaps, and he plugs them. It's the combination of the seeing and the doing which characterises the entrepreneur.

Surinder was always alert to opportunities and kept his eyes and ears open. With his wide community links through his jobs and his mother, he had a good sense of what was going on and eventually spotted a gap in the market. His love of planes and work with British Airways had set the foundations. He realized that British Airways booked several different hotels for its crew, and decided to build an airport hotel solely for aircrew. He realized that 'other hotels want crew when they are not full, but at peak times it is a hassle for them. Crew normally receive in the region of a 50 percent discount on the room rate. This is fine if a hotel is not at full capacity.' He decided to specialize and has now expanded to catering for mixed crew from all airlines, not just British Airways.

He needed land to build his hotel on, and even today in his boardroom there is a display of photographs of the original shabby old houses that were the foundations of the first Arora hotel. He is nostalgic, and seeing the derelict houses inspires him as they were his first steps into the big time. Success was not easy and Surinder encountered many hurdles when he first set out to build his hotel empire. Having found the site, 'I had to buy these derelict houses from nine different owners. That was not easy'. He had to use all his negotiating skills and it required a lot of stamina dealing with and convincing a multitude of owners to sell. This was a complex operation with so many stakeholders. The next step was to get planning permission to knock them down and build a hotel. This was just not happening. The planners said 'no' and a long wrangle ensued. It was a further two years before Surinder got over that hurdle.

He then had to approach British Airways to offer them the services of his unique hotel which was the first purpose-built hotel for crew. He did not make a good first impression. 'I was an unknown entity,' he recalls. It was important for BA to ensure that their crew were well looked after to ensure flight safety; the Civil Aviation Authority had strict guidelines on hours of sleep required by crew, and Surinder was just too much of an unknown. How could they take that risk with him? He had no credibility. The banks didn't support him either: 'I had no track record of building a hotel or running one'.

Surinder remembers this challenging period in his life. 'The site I found had nine different owners when I bought it. I struggled, got planning permission eventually, went to BA and again struggled to convince them.' At that time, many people with lesser mettle would have given up. Surinder recalls, 'Even my bank manager said to me, "Sell and retire". He warned me about the hotel, it was too risky. "What do you know about hotels?" he kept asking me.' Today, the banks who were reluctant to lend to him in the early days are queuing up to see him. He was determined, all the setbacks made him even more resolute. He had to prove to everyone, including his family and the banks, that he could do it.

He never gave up. Despite the setbacks, the closed doors and the utter despondency he persevered. He says, 'It's important to talk to people, to listen to them and to value their advice no matter whom, but at the end of the day make your own decisions.' He did. He eventually over came all of the barriers and the hotel was set up and ready for business. He then had to go on to deliver, once it was ready.

Rising Star

Ever-expansive and entrepreneurial, Surinder brought in a team to deal with the detail: 'I have to delegate and trust, but I am hands-on. I know what's going on but I respect their space'. He surrounds himself with a strong team which includes several family members.

It was an important step. By now he was running a large outfit with employees and having to take responsibility for it all. It was a steep learning curve but with dogged determination, he was ready for the challenge and was a natural at dealing with employees. In what little spare time he had he recalls, 'Football refereeing is the biggest thing that helped me in terms of running a large organization. I used to get on the pitch with my red and yellow cards, determined to do a good job, until a fellow referee told me to relax and enjoy myself.' His golden rule is, 'If I walk on the pitch with 22 players, I want to walk off with 22 players.' Respect is mutual with employees, too. 'I want their respect and I want to give them mine. It's a two way thing,' says Surinder.

'It's the same in business, my first employee was my general manager who had come from Trusthouse Forte. I wanted to be different. I wanted to be hands on, to know what's going on, and to know all my staff.' He expects all his managers to treat everyone well and equally, be they porters, maids or senior executives. 'In the hotel business, it's so important that all your staff are courteous, the front-line staff in particular. The porter is the first person a guest is going to see, the maid is seen every day and just a friendly "hello" from them makes a difference,' he says, explaining the merits of his classless approach.

He wants to promote a culture within the organization where every-one is treated as part of the family. 'I recruit employees who have the "Arora DNA". I need two-way traffic, I need 100 percent from them and I will give back 110 percent,' he says. The pecking order is your own immediate family first and the Arora business family second. One female employee who has worked for him for over two years has sadly been diagnosed with cancer. He stresses, 'We, as a company, regardless of statutory regulations, are continuing to pay her a full salary. I pre-fer giving back to the community in this way rather than writing an anonymous cheque to a charity.'

The Arora International was the first hotel in the group and now there are 14 others, including the Gatwick Hilton. Some the Group operate themselves, others are owned in a family trust. The Penta hotel where Surinder first worked later changed hands and became the Renaissance, and Surinder now owns the very hotel he was work-ing in during the early part of his working life. Similarly, he has just bought the flying club where he first learnt to fly. In life you can't do everything yourself. He feels: 'You work either as a hunter or a farmer. My choice is to be a farmer. I plough away.'

Loyalty is important to Surinder. 'I have kept the same relationships for years. I have stayed with the Allied Irish Bank and Royal Bank of Scotland because they helped me at the start.' It is worth financial institutions expending the time and resources in building relation-ships with their Asian customers and building trust and rapport, as this investment may be repaid manifold. 'I have been with them since day one. I have built up a relationship and track record. I negotiate hard. But I treat them like an extended family. The same holds true for the lawyers.' Relationships are important. 'I don't chop and change but I do negotiate... I won't leave over just a few pounds, the relationships are worth more than that.' As a skilled negotiator, Surinder demon-strates another of the key facets of the Asian entrepreneurial mindset.

Surinder also has a knack of engaging with people, regardless of who they are. He wanted an organization promoting the best of different cultures.

For example, his wheelchair-bound, 32-year-old switchboard attendant has excelled in the job. When he first started and received his first pay cheque he cried. No one had given him a job before. 'I give to charities in the UK and India and orphanages but I like to see what I can do for people around me,' says this hands-on entrepreneur. Surinder instils loyalty from his staff, and in a sector where employee turnover is notoriously high, his is very low. Despite his growing empire he knows his employees by name and works longer hours than the majority of them.

A Joint Venture with the Bachelor Boy

This boy from the Punjab has made friends with a Lucknow boy – Cliff Richard. They first met when Cliff opened the first Arora hotel in memory of Surinder's mother who had sadly passed away: 'I wanted someone famous to open it and a British Airways Director suggested Cliff Richard.' They have been long-standing friends ever since, so much so that they are in partnership together in a hotel they bought in Manchester. Each of them could have gone it alone but they felt it was a good marriage of experience and show business. The hotel boasts Cliff-themed bedrooms and original memorabilia donated by the singer. In addition, Cliff makes a point of meeting the hotel staff in person at least twice a year.

They purchased the hotel while it was still incomplete. The original owner was having difficulty in completing the project and was looking for a way out. In walked Surinder and Cliff.

Persistence Pays

Surinder says, 'In life if you want something you have to pay the price for it. I consoled myself that I was doing everything for the family. I am ambitious but I never forget my roots. Look one step ahead but don't forget your roots. Opportunities are available but not everyone wants them. People limit themselves.' He reflects on the British attitude to success. 'In the UK, if someone sees you doing well they say, "how can I get you out of there?" In the US they would say, "how can I get myself in there?" There's a big difference in attitudes to success.'

There is a lot of jealousy here in the UK. In the early days Surinder remembers the racism, which was especially faced by the first generation. Even now there are very few black or Asian faces at the highest levels in organizations. 'You have to work twice as hard to get a promotion if you're Asian, ' he says. The 70s were a particularly difficult time for the immigrant community in the UK; they were seen as a threat and treated with hostility and disdain. Many doors were closed to them and they had to overcome barriers through sheer hard work. Surinder's advice is, 'Keep at it, and don't walk away'. Persistence pays. And, for him, it did... 'I love the view from my office, the putting green, the planes, the giant boardroom.'

Still in his prime, Surinder has built his empire. His hotel group currently comprises some 5500 rooms including the Arora International, Heathrow; Arora Park, Heathrow; Arora International, Gatwick/Crawley; Arora International, Manchester; Sofitel, London Gatwick and Sofitel London Heathrow (at Terminal 5, opening Spring 2008) and he employs over 500 people. In terms of giving back to the community, Surinder joined a couple of government boards last year concerned with skills and employment. He says, 'It seems wrong to me. The systems are so overly complicated, there are so many government bodies involved. Everything is so confusing and long winded.'

His hobbies include golf and football. 'I miss flying planes,' he admits. He loves cricket and not surprisingly says, 'I am about to build a hotel in the Oval soon!' Arora International Hotels announced in January 2007 that it is to open a 170-bed four-star hotel there in time for the Ashes in 2009. Surinder, a keen golfer, lives a stone's throw away from Wentworth and has recently acquired a minority interest in the Wentworth Golf Club. Richard Caring, the clothing magnate and fellow entrepreneur, holds the majority holding in the prestigious club and they seem to have a strong partnership.

Vince Lombardi, one of the most successful coaches in the history of American football, once said 'the harder you work, the harder it is to surrender'. Propelled by an extraordinary drive and an ambitious mother, there is no denying the stamina and determination of Surinder and, in a passionate tribute to his mother, he says, 'My natural mother is my inspiration and driver. She was my best friend. She helped me and pushed me. She was my driving force.' He concedes, 'She was a hard taskmaster but she had common sense in abundance.' His mother used her contacts and knew how to open doors for him and was always protective of his interests. 'I am not afraid of hard work. I watched my parents work night and day and I have certainly done it'. The time between the ages of 13 and 18 was the most crucial in his life and laid down the foundations and ethos for the rest of his life and success. He admits he has not spent as much time with his family as he would have wanted to but says, 'whatever you decide to do, there is a price to pay'. His family have remained supportive and are enjoying the fruits of their sacrifice.

Surinder has succeeded in creating the biggest family-run independent hotel chain in Britain. His hotel and property empire have prospered through sheer hard work. With no concrete career plan, Surinder had opportunism and determination in abundance. For one so young, he is comfortable with his success, and for someone who has achieved enviable success in a relatively short period of time he wears it well. He is a charismatic man, no one's fool, shrewd and easy going. He has not forgotten his roots and shows no sign of arrogance: 'I keep my head down and I try not to be big headed.' He has nothing to prove. After all, as he says, 'The taller the tree, the less fruit grows on it!'

Background Reading

BBC News. 'Hotel chain is a hit with Cliff', *BBC News/Merseyside*, April 16, 2004.

Davidson, A., 'The Andrew Davidson Interview, Arora: A tycoon with drive', *Sunday Times*, March 26, 2006.

Lord Karan Bilimoria

Photo supplied by Karan Bilimoria

From Brunel University's presentation of Honorary Doctor of Business to Lord Karan Bilimoria in July 2005:

'An unstoppable character who negotiates brewing in Bangalore and importing to the United Kingdom, who cold-calls on Indian restaurants and supermarkets with cases of the beer in his tiny Citroën, and who turns these unpropitious beginnings during a recession into a prize-winning, fast-growing company and a global brand with continuous penetration of new international markets is certainly a person who encapsulates the romance, challenge and triumphs of entrepreneurship.'

Chapter 3

Karan Faridoon Bilimoria is one of the UK's most popular and recognized entrepreneurs. His commitment to championing enterprise and entrepreneurship coupled with his contributions in giving back to the community led to his being appointed as a crossbench peer in the House of Lords. But it is for founding Cobra Beer that Karan is best known. The company was started in 1989, when Karan was 27 years old and still had £20,000 of student debt. Since then Karan and Cobra have gone from strength to strength. Cobra is stocked in Indian restaurants the length and breadth of the country and is also now available in over 6000 bars, pubs and clubs and more than 5000 supermarkets. Headquartered in London, Karan has set up further Cobra offices in Mumbai and Cape Town and now brews in five countries including the UK and India. Cobra is now one of Britain's fastest growing beer brands, and has been exported to almost 50 countries worldwide.

Breaking the Mould

With his clipped British accent, his Cambridge education and his seat in the House of Lords, Karan Bilimoria smacks of good breeding. This media-savvy businessman, still in his early forties, has done much to both promote Asian entrepreneurship in the UK and to strengthen trade links between India and the UK. Deeper enquiry, however, reveals that although the Bilimoria family may have the status of a wealthy Indian family, they once lacked the ready cash. Karan Bilimoria was born and brought up in India in a series of boarding schools, finishing at Lushington Hall, where most pupils are British expatriates and which he needed special permission to attend. He read for a degree in commerce at Osmania University in Hyderabad.

Karan's paternal grandfather was a great influence on him in his early years and advised Karan not to go into the army, as was the family tradition, but to become a professional. Karan contemplated a military career but felt he would always be in the shadow of his father, who was Commander-in-Chief of the Central Indian Army. His father had always been a great inspiration, but he was determined to make his own way. Freedom means a lot to Karan, and he wanted to carve out a career for himself. His father was not happy about this as he had expected Karan to follow in his footsteps. Instead Karan came to London to study to be an accountant. His early days in Britain were not lived in the lavish lifestyle he is now able to enjoy; he stayed in a YMCA on Fitzroy Square in London and was funded by a combination of grants and family handouts. It was here that the young Bilimoria got an inkling for an idea which was later to catapult him to entrepreneurial success. 'I came up with the idea for Cobra Beer when I was still a student,' Karan recalls. The YMCA was surrounded by Indian restaurants and it was here that Karan first discovered European lagers. He was not impressed: 'I found them gassy, very fizzy and very bland.' Like most business ideas the conception of Cobra came from a disappointing consumer experience and thinking, 'maybe I could do better and do it differently – maybe I could change the market forever'. At that time in Britain, lager followed by an Indian curry was a national pastime on a Friday or Saturday night. An idea had formed in his mind.

But first he embarked on a career in chartered accountancy, qualifying with Arthur Young (now Ernst & Young). This exposed him to a variety of businesses of all shapes and sizes, giving Karan a privileged view of life on the other side of the audit fence. 'Accountancy training is primarily training in business, where as an auditor you are privileged to learn about business from within businesses,' explains Karan. 'Accountancy is basically a people business and, what is more, it is the strong principles, values and ethics that are the cornerstone of the profession – we are always taught not just to do things right, but more importantly to always do the right thing.' He gained a wealth of experience during his time with the company and this was to be of great value to him in his own business later. As bestselling motivational author Napoleon Hill said, 'Experience is an asset of which no worker can be cheated'. Like most entrepreneurs, Karan did not enjoy working for such a large organization but appreciated the discipline it instilled in him. Having to deal with clients in often difficult situations was a valuable lesson in the need for strong interpersonal skills in business, and Karan is well known today for his excellent negotiation and sales skills.

He soon went to study law at Cambridge University and threw himself headfirst into student life, picking up some useful entrepreneurial skills along the way. At Cambridge it dawned on him that he could sell; he had to go door to door canvassing to get himself elected to the Union. His sales patter paid off and he was elected vice president. Later on, he would look back at this period with gratitude for the learning experience as he went from restaurant to restaurant trying to sell his lager; the early years of training paid good dividends. He flourished at Cambridge, not only joining the prestigious debating society, but also becoming an accomplished polo player.

What's the Big Idea?

After completing his degree at Cambridge, Karan was set to enter the world of corporate finance. However, his leanings towards entrepreneurship and his love of polo got in the way. He was committed to a polo tour in India and couldn't resist bringing back some sample polo sticks: 'I considered Indian-made polo sticks to be made differently to those in the UK.' They are lighter and made from bamboo heads which last forever; English polo sticks are made from willow heads which tend to split. Not all his entrepreneurial ideas were successful, but the next thing he knew he was putting his selling skills to good use. Never having lacked ambition, the green Karan did manage to sell his wares, but not without some opposition. 'I tried to get my polo sticks into Harrods and they wouldn't even see me as I didn't have a company,' he recalls. He persisted and did manage to convince a buyer at Harrods to place an order and also sold them to Lillywhites and Gidden's, the royal family's saddlers. Enterprise was not lauded the way it is today. Karan recalls that, in his Cambridge days, entrepreneurship as it is known today did not exist; only the professions were valued. Entrepreneurship had a 'wide boy' image. 'Perhaps it's no coincidence that Britain at that time was the "sick man" of Europe,' says Karan.

But the spirit of the entrepreneur was about to explode. Karan finished his degree and was £20,000 in debt. His heart was not in working for financial services in the city; he wanted more action. Enterprise beckoned. Cue Arjun Reddy, his long-term friend and the start of A&K International. This was formed in 1986 by Karan Bilimoria and Arjun Reddy and is where the Cobra story really begins. Both men were born and brought up in India in affluent surroundings. Whilst Karan's father, grandfather and great grandfather all had military backgrounds, his mother's side were in business in the old state of Hyderabad, building a substantial conglomerate embracing interests as diverse as rice, property and the cinema. Arjun too came from an old and powerful Hyderabadi family. His father was well educated, with a law degree, and became the Chief of Justice.

The next step was not easy. Karan had always felt that he would set up in business later on in life when he had accumulated the necessary capital. However, he was urged on by friends who said to him that he had the necessary qualifications and experience, so what was he waiting for? He also saw his younger brother doing very well in an advertising business that he had started from scratch in a field in which he had no previous experience, and so Karan mustered up the courage to take the plunge to start his own business.

As Earl Wilson once said, 'Success is simply a matter of luck. Ask any failure.' Karan and Arjun did not want to rely on luck. They went to India, researched products that they could market and made a list of all their contacts there. When they returned to England they established exactly who their contacts were and how they could pursue their goals. They made an attempt to import polo sticks at first, then leather goods, before eventually settling on beer. They had started the business with virtually no money. The problem was that dealing with their suppliers in India was not easy; some of the polo sticks were faulty and their quality could not be relied upon. They needed another idea. The other, more personal, problem Karan faced was that his parents despaired that their son was selling polo sticks. This was not the future they had mapped out for their boy.

Then, through luck as much as good judgement, Karan and Arjun decided to import seafood from a company called Pals. After closer examination of the brochure they found they were less interested in Pals' seafood and more in Pals' beer, which was a division of the Mysore Brewery. The Mysore brewery was a former Coca-Cola bottling plant and had grown to become the biggest privately owned brewer in India; India has over 40 breweries and a 150-year-old brewing tradition. Karan and Arjun had longstanding connections with Mysore Breweries and so they persuaded Mysore to come up with a new brew. A Czech influence was imparted by a brewmaster who had previously worked with Pilsner Urquell. This, together with Danish technology that had been installed by Carlsberg 25 years previously, meant that A&K International benefited from taking the best from the Czechs and Danes, the acknowledged world kings of beer. The Danes oversaw the process for the first year and then it was turned over to India completely. Water came from the brewery's own spring, the malt from Punjab and Haryana, and the yeast was the brewery's own strain; only the hops were imported. An attempt was made to grow them in Kashmir, but this had to be abandoned after they were burned by terrorists.

The start to the negotiations was done in a typically entrepreneurial way by Karan. As things got underway, however, the problems escalated. Karan became increasingly frustrated trying to communicate with their contacts in India – so much so that he jumped on a plane and went to India to talk face to face. Karan was 28 years old when he met Mr Balan, owner and managing director of Mysore Breweries in Bangalore. It was his first taste of corporate deal-making and negotiation, but if he was daunted sitting in the hot seat in front of a group of executives he didn't show it. Meetings, in an Asian setting, often include many people, some in their corporate role, others because they are relatives or elders and need to be consulted out of duty and respect. It is important to establish who the key influencers are. Karan was shrewd enough to recognise them. If Asians are well known for being skilled negotiators, then Karan is one of the best. He made a convincing pitch with evident self-belief, passion and confidence to a sceptical audience and made the deal of his life. He secured the brewing contract. Ecstatic with this success, he turned to his next challenge. He used his network of family contacts to get in touch with big bottle manufacturers.

Trouble Brewing

Winston Churchill once said, 'Courage is going from failure to failure without losing enthusiasm'. Whilst not failing, A&K International were to encounter several problems. There was a lot of red tape to deal with before they could get samples out of India and into the UK. They finally managed to get them freighted – however, many of the bottles were broken by the time they landed in the UK, thus rendering the exercise useless. Karan managed to persuade a friend to bring a few bottles in his hand luggage. There was also the issue of branding the product: the name 'Pals' was too closely associated with dog food in the UK. They had to create a brand of their own. The recipes were not what Karan wanted so the Mysore brewery had to produce an entirely new recipe to their specifications.

Another major stumbling block was dealing with the excise authorities in India, which insisted that bottles be labelled with the state where the beer was to be sold. Cobra was brewed in the state of Karnataka, but for export, so Karan was obliged to write 'not for sale in Karnataka, for export only' on each bottle. Of course he did not want to write all that as it took up valuable space on the label and would be meaningless to UK customers. It took all his persuasive skills but he eventually managed to convince the authorities of this. The final panic was the original name of the product: Panther. None of the distributors liked the name. He then had to check whether the labels had been printed; luckily they hadn't. Family connections are the backbone of Asian entrepreneurial success, and this story is no different. Karan went to his brother, Nadir, who was based in Hyderabad and had founded an advertising agency. Within two weeks the brothers had designed the new label from scratch and Cobra was born.

The next biggest challenge was raising finance. Cobra Beer got under way in one of the worst recessions since the war. The base rate was 14 percent, banks had clamped down on lending – it was not a good time to be starting up in business. The real challenge, however, was to raise money 'in a way which meant we could protect and hold on to the ownership of our business', according to Karan. Ever resourceful, he used both imagination and determination to reach his goal. His accountancy background was important. He took on a large overdraft and a £55,000 loan through a government-backed loan scheme. He also used his community contacts, in particular Gandhi Oriental Foods in Bow, East London, who acted as distributors for Cobra. Cobra had no credit rating so they made an arrangement with Gandhi, whose company credit rating was impeccable.

The 'Indian' restaurants (many are Bengali) are to be credited for paving the way for many an Asian entrepreneur. They were expanding rapidly in the UK and becoming a familiar sight in every high street. They certainly paved the way for Karan's business and were the initial base for Cobra. Karan had the odds stacked against him, apart from

being new in the Indian restaurant marketplace – which already had
established beers in place – Cobra also faced a problem with its bottles. The snag was the size of the bottles. In the UK the regular size is
330 ml, but in India it is 650 ml. Indian restaurant customers were
more used to the smaller bottles. Ever quick to turn a negative into a
positive, Karan used his sales acumen and pointed out to his potential
customers just how authentic this method was of drinking the beer,
and the benefits of the sharing aspects of one bottle and two glasses.
It worked, and he started making sales.

Haggling is probably one of the most interesting and at the same time
frustrating aspects of the Asian culture. It's a matter of course; Asians
must come out of any deal or negotiation feeling they have won, or
that they have got something out of it. If you understand this aspect
of the culture you can set yourself up for negotiation. Asians are
skilled negotiators, they are negotiators par excellence, and this can be
irritating for people who are not used to it. Some people take it as a
personal affront, others think it is preposterous. But once the haggling
is finished and the deal is done, the relationship is just as strong as it
was before; it's not personal.

Image is everything. Karan and Arjun had priced their beer at the premium end of the market and were careful, in the early days, to park their
battered Citroen 2CV several streets away and out of sight before carrying cases to restaurant owners. Recalling his humble start Karan
explains, 'I had an old car and we used to park it down the road from the
restaurants we were delivering to.' He bought this Citroen 2CV for £295,
money borrowed from Arjun. Despite their shabby transport, they were
both confident of their product and were not willing to compromise on
price; they held firm. Once again, Karan's selling skills were tested to the
hilt when he had to go from restaurant to restaurant to convince the
owners, many of whom were teetotal, of the merit of his product.

When Napoleon Hill wrote, 'Patience, persistence and perspiration
make an unbeatable combination for success,' he could have been

referring to Karan and Arjun. It was to be another five years of hard work and struggle before their revenue reached £1 million. Karan recalls feeling very demoralised during that period but never contemplated giving up. Arjun decided otherwise, leaving the company in 1995 to return to India and pursue other avenues once everything was in place. This left Karan as the sole owner and ready for the next phase in this entrepreneurial success story. The departure of Arjun was a key turning point and led to the professionalization of the company, sparking a new stage of development and the emergence of a management team. Growth was steady but the company needed to develop to keep up with this demand and Karan had to sell shares in the company to raise £500,000 in investment. He was later to caution others to try and get finance without losing equity, a fine balance.

Despite the gradual acceptance of his beer, Karan found that importing the beer from India was swallowing up 50 percent of management time in organization and administration. The solution was to brew in Britain.

A Bright Future

After much deliberation Karan went with the Bedford-based, family-owned firm Charles Wells (now Wells & Young's), which also makes Jamaican Red Stripe and Japanese Kirin Beer. After several attempts to get the formula right, it is now producing a draught form of the beer which is available in close to 3000 outlets. Whereas for many years Cobra lager was only available in Indian restaurants, today they are far from being the only place you can enjoy the beer. Now it's available in all major supermarkets, off licences and in a rapidly increasing number of pubs and bars across the UK. There is no stopping this man and as for the future, Karan sees plenty of opportunities for growth apart from the obvious further expansion into the export market. He sees the potential in pubs and clubs too.

No man is an island, and Karan credits his employees for being the great team he needs. His philosophy is always to hire the best people and to work with the best advisors and this formula has certainly paid dividends. He has always used the media to full effect and has expended a lot of time, effort and resources in marketing Cobra, learning early on that marketing was invaluable to the success and sustainability of his product. He hired only the best and, at times, was accused of being extravagant. Team Saatchi, the advertising agency responsible for Cobra's first major campaign, won four awards for the advertising campaign they created. When Karan first started out in the very competitive beer market people found it incredible. He was trying to enter an already overcrowded market with a beer brewed in India when Britain had pubs in virtually every corner of every town and city. It was quite courageous and headlines such as 'selling coal to Newcastle' appeared.

Near Collapse

Karan's innovative approach to marketing is the key to his success. To increase the Cobra profile further, he helped to create *Tandoori* magazine, which was a touch of genius. It was a trade magazine going to all the restaurants he wanted to target – the first of its kind for the sector – and so it kept the profile of Cobra high. His then-PR manager Iqbal Wahhab was given the job of editor. *Tandoori* had a brilliant marketing strategy, selling directly to restaurants, and was launched in September 1994 with Karan as the publisher.

However, it was to nearly be his undoing four years later. On February 19, 1998, Iqbal had his 'Ratners moment' and wrote an article criticising standards in Indian restaurants. The restaurant owners were outraged at this slur and Cobra sales plummeted. There was a disciplined, well-organised boycott of his product and Wahhab resigned. A real leader faces the music, even when he doesn't like the tune. Karan showed true grit and took action. He wrote a 2000-word apology in the next issue of *Tandoori*, but it was a long time before sales crept up again.

Karan was faced with another blow years later when he had Team Saatchi overseeing Cobra's advertising. They were expensive but the results were excellent and the ads won awards. He was shocked, then, when Saachi's dumped him due to a conflict of interest with Carlsberg Tetley. It was a bitter blow. But at least now he figured he was a threat to the big boys. He had made his mark.

Making a Fortune – the Bilimoria Way

Entrepreneurs are often great with ideas and not so great with the detail. According to Karan, the key to running a successful business is to be able to delegate, and the real secret to success is to employ people better than you and to trust and respect them. He knows his own strengths lie in production, sales, marketing and finance, but concedes his directors '...are way better than me'. The best piece of management advice he received was when he got his first job at Ernst & Young, and his father told him, 'Whenever you are given a task, the first thing is to do it. The second thing is to always do that little bit extra. Be innovative, be creative and go the extra mile.' He encourages innovation and creativity in his team too. He has an open office culture which fosters interaction, the sharing of ideas and an enthusiasm for taking responsibility and turning vision into actuality. The proof is in the pudding and Cobra boasts a low staff turnover, with some of his former employees returning to the company professing to miss the energy and the stimulating buzz. This is further illustrated by his company having the prestigious 'Investors in People' certification, and it has also been ranked by the *Sunday Times* as one of the 100 best small companies to work for in the UK from 2004 to 2007.

Karan stresses the importance of the company's values and beliefs. In particular, with a large proportion of its employees and consumers coming from an Asian background, Karan highlights and recognises the importance of what he calls 'Asian values' such as hard work, education and family values. Cobra has very few rules, and that trust is

rewarded by absolute professionalism from its team. The team is eth-
nically diverse, with staff from over 20 countries. This diverse and
open culture at Cobra ensures that, in a fast-moving environment, all
departments are able to work together to fully achieve the company's
goals. The company aims to work in a fully integrated manner, not in
individual or departmental silos.

Karan's advice to would-be entrepreneurs is, 'Have a vision. It's important to be passionate about what you do: it will never be easy and you
will need focus, determination and guts.' He continues, 'Be different,
be better, and change the marketplace forever.' Or, in the words of
Winston Churchill, 'Never give in, never give in, never give in'.

Corporate Social Responsibility – a Winning Formula

Karan certainly enjoys a high profile within Britain's Asian community
and is regularly seen at key events. He interconnects his community
and business in a way that makes good business sense and helps charities. Over the years, Cobra Beer has given away thousands of pounds
of beer and wine at a variety of charitable events. But this generosity
also serves as a good marketing opportunity. 'It's a win-win situation,'
Karan explains. He also supports a number of charities and acts as a
business adviser. It is his commitment to championing enterprise and
entrepreneurship coupled with his contributions to the community
that led to his being appointed as a crossbench peer in the House of
Lords in 2006. He uses this role as a great ambassador for the Asian
business community and champions budding entrepreneurs. Karan is
a polished and powerful speaker.

So what next? Karan is quick to defend his product despite the general decline in the UK beer market; he insists that the world beer sector
is not declining. A flotation of the company is expected in the near
future but he insists that this is not an exit route. It is difficult to think
of Cobra without Karan at its helm, '...one of the biggest barriers to
growth for entrepreneurs', he says, 'is the challenge of letting go.'

Aware of this and the attractiveness of his company to others, 'I believe in the brand and the future of the business,' he claims, confidently. He is reluctant to sell his own shares and this is proving more difficult as his profile and that of the company grows. 'People want to buy shares in my company,' he asserts, but so far he has refused. This proprietorial attitude is understandable and is typical of many Asian entrepreneurs who are reluctant to let go of the business even if this stifles growth. Karan is the chairman and 67 percent shareholder of Cobra Beer Limited, but a listing for Cobra is highly likely.

Without doubt a success story, Cobra Beer is one of the fastest growing beer brands in the UK. It has been exported to almost 50 countries worldwide, and is available nationwide in more than 6000 Indian restaurants, major supermarkets and off-licences and now mainstream bars, pubs and clubs. Cobra Beer was awarded six Grand Gold Medals and fourteen Gold Medals at the 2007 Monde Selection, Brussels – World Selection of Quality. That's the most in the world awarded to a beer brand for the third consecutive year. And, among numerous other accolades, Cobra was listed on the 1999 Virgin Fast Track 100 list of the fastest growing privately owned companies in the UK.

Never one to rest on his laurels, Karan launched the General Bilimoria Wines brand in 1999. He named his wine range after his father, perhaps as a consolation for not following him into the army. With 125 employees in the UK and a further 175 worldwide, (particularly in India and South Africa), the company continues to go from strength to strength. It is unlikely that this man, with his relentless energy and self-belief, will stop here. Karan has ambitious plans for further growth of the brand, particularly in India and Britain. Proud of his Parsi roots and Indian heritage, he promotes commercial and cultural relations between the United Kingdom and the Asian subcontinent. He honours the importance of friendship and community, of warmth and family. He is married to Heather who he credits for being 'very understanding' and has two sons and two daughters. In June 2006, Karan was appointed Lord Bilimoria of Chelsea. The entrepreneurial

world will see much more of this man in his early forties, who remains
a workaholic and who still routinely puts in an 18-hour day. His company motto is 'to aspire and achieve against all the odds, with integrity.'
He has.

Background Reading

Bilimoria, K., with Coomber, S., *Bottled For Business: The Less Gassy Guide to
  Entrepreneurship*, Capstone Publishing Ltd, 2007.
Benjamin, A., 'Leading questions: Lord (Karan) Bilimoria', *Guardian*, Feb. 14,
  2007.
Brunel University, Citation Conferment of Doctor in Business, Karan
  Bilimoria, July 2005.
Clark, E., 'The "less gassy" rise of Cobra Beer', *BBC Online Business Reporter*,
  Aug. 21, 2003.
Fielding, R., 'Profile: Cobra beer king Karan Bilimoria', *Accountancy Age*, May
  11, 2005.
Woodward, D., 'Karan Bilimoria', *Director*, March 2007.

Dinesh Dhamija

Reproduced by permission of Dinesh Dhamija

Golf enthusiast and Cambridge graduate Dinesh Dhamija founded ebookers.com travel, the UK's first commercially interactive internet company, which later became one of Europe's most successful and well known entrepreneurial companies. Dinesh, the son of an Indian diplomat, came to the UK in 1968 and holds a Master of Arts degree in Law from Cambridge University. After a spell at various companies, including IBM, he started his own rise in business in 1980 with a small kiosk in Earls Court station in west London, named Dabin Travel, selling cheap flights to budget travellers. This was followed in 1983 by Flightbookers plc, which grew to be one of the UK's largest leisure travel agencies. In 1996, while heading Flightbookers, Dinesh was instrumental in the company's setting up of a fully interactive travel website and was to become Chairman and Chief Executive Officer of ebookers.com in 1999. The company was to endure the dotcom bubble bursting, the September 11 attacks, the war in Iraq and the SARS epidemic, and still survive. Dinesh sold ebookers.com to Cedant in 2005. After a brief stint of focusing on property and private equity in India, he turned his attention to property development in Romania. The Copper Beech Group is now the largest residential property developer in Romania, responsible for building over 16,600 dwellings. He is married to Tani and they have two sons, Biren and Darun. Dinesh is easily worth an estimated £200 million.

Chapter 4

Travel Bug

Driving through the stunning Surrey countryside, it's impossible not to be taken in by the romantic scenery all around, the peace and quiet. Virginia Water, one of the UK's most beautiful and exclusive areas, boasts the Wentworth golf club and is a fitting place to be one of the residences of Dinesh Dhamija. Its appeal becomes even more apparent when you enter his house, tastefully decorated throughout and with views of his private tennis court and swimming pool. The grounds are immaculate and well tended by his bevy of workers.

As the son of an Indian diplomat, Dinesh's childhood was spent changing countries every three years. Born in Australia, he grew up in India, Mauritius, Afghanistan, Czechoslovakia and Holland. For one so well travelled at an early age, he has an interesting archive of memories. He recalls an eventful period in Mauritius when he was just 10 years old: 'There were two cyclones, one in January called Alex and the other in March called Carol.' The episode made a deep impression. 'Carol's winds were 200 miles per hour and half the roof on our house flew off during the night.' It was a poignant memory. 'I was terrified,' he recalls with fervour. On a more peaceful note, he also remembers being mesmerised by 'the beautiful lakes in Mazar-i-Sharif and the giant Buddhas in Bamiyan in Afghanistan.' Given that start in life, he was probably destined to open a travel agency. This prophecy was given further credence by his marriage to an airline stewardess, Tani.

Dinesh left Cambridge University with an MA in Law in 1974 and no idea what to do. For the next five years he worked for three companies including IBM. In 1979 he finally realized that he was not made to work for others. The job was enjoyable enough but he was increasingly frustrated at the amount of tax that was leaving his pay packet. He earned a modest salary of just over £7000 per annum but this was a period of high taxation under the then Labour government and Dinesh recalls, 'I was paying 40 percent tax and a further 10 percent national insurance, that meant I was losing half my salary!' He was not happy with this and it was a key driver to his first steps into entrepreneurship. 'This spurred me to set up my own business,' he says firmly, 'I wanted to keep the money I had made.' But there were several other factors that he found helped him decide to go it alone and set up in business. Firstly, he realized that as a self-employed person, he could offset many of his expenses against the business in order to reduce the amount of tax paid. 'I liked the idea of being rewarded for my efforts and controlling the amount of tax I paid.' Secondly, 'you can earn a lot more money in business if you are successful, rather than just a monthly salary, there is no upper limit.' This was very attractive to him and finally, he says, 'most people talk about "risk" and not "benefits". There are a lot of benefits to being self-employed.' He argues, 'We should talk more about the benefits of entrepreneurship and less about the risks.'

The travel industry was attractive and familiar to both Tani and Dinesh, and the impetus for a travel agency came from his wife. Tani, as was the rule in those days, had to resign as an air stewardess following her marriage, and by now they had two sons. They had no savings and so borrowed a small amount of money from friends to open up a travel kiosk in a hole in the wall in Earls Court tube station. This was 1980 and the travel agency was named Dabin travel, after their two sons, Darun and Biren. Dinesh is an entrepreneur, however: 'there's really no reason why it had to be travel. It really could have been anything. If I could sell it, and make money selling it then I would have done it,' he declares. By 1983 they had established

Flightbookers, an IATA travel agency which soon expanded to three premises.

Hard work never killed anyone and, not being one to rest on his laurels, Dinesh's passion for travel developed further when in 1987 he was appointed as General Sales Agent (GSA) for Royal Nepal Airlines for the UK and Ireland. For the next six years he worked consecutively as European GSA for Air Botswana, Zambia Airways, Air Tanzania and Royal Nepal Airlines. In 1993 Dinesh was appointed as Regional Director for Europe for Royal Nepal Airlines where his responsibilities included running the sales, marketing and airport support functions. During this time he developed the sales function for a network of travel agencies in 12 European countries to support Royal Nepal's flights to London, Frankfurt and Paris. This was to prove extremely valuable later on - these contacts were to stand him in good stead setting up the ebookers.com operation across Europe. By 1996 Flightbookers had grown into one of the UK's top ten leisure travel agencies.

'Luck is an important part of success,' professes Dinesh. And Lady Luck bought a German colleague his way who was to transform Dinesh's fortunes to a level he could not have imagined.

The Internet Revolution

It was in the mid 1990s that things really took off for Dinesh. His travel business was doing well but he had even bigger ambitions. He had always taken a macro view of the business, not wanting to be limited to the UK. Having travelled so widely in his early days, his vision was far reaching. 'It's easier for me to look at the wider world', he explains, 'with no inhibitions about a global network.' He saw his opportunity when the German associate introduced him to an innovative IT software package which enabled online bookings and transactions. Bookings had been manual prior to this - agents took bookings which had to be reserved through the specific airlines who then would come back and confirm the booking. It was a cumbersome, tedious and time-consuming process, but this was the way the travel industry had always operated. The new software would enable bookings to be confirmed online. It was quickly installed and Flightbookers.com became the first interactive travel website in the UK - a real internet pioneer.

When the software was first introduced to him, Dinesh was wary. It had suffered some teething problems but, by the time it was incorporated by Flightbookers in 1996, it had been refined and the earlier problems dealt with. Dinesh soon began to see the benefits when the orders rolled in, although not everyone in the company was convinced. Other staff were afraid that jobs would go and that they would be replaced by computers. There was scepticism from other quarters too, as this was new, unproven technology and change is threatening; people disliked things they were unfamiliar with. Dinesh knew that to master the system and to make it pay dividends, firm action would have to be taken. Not one to shy away from a challenge, Dinesh left as managing director of Flightbookers and started the new company for which he was soon to become a major global player, ebookers.com. Instigating change is never easy: 'the old order had to be swept away with the new.' He found the challenge exhilarating. 'For once, I was on the crest of a wave of change rather than a follower', he says.

Undaunted by the new technology, he led his team forward with gusto, keeping them motivated and enthused. Ebookers.com was based in Central London and employees were accommodated in open-plan offices. The benefits of this were threefold, according to Dinesh: 'you make better use of available space, it reduces clutter and thus offices are tidier and it's easier for people to communicate if they need to immediately.' Any private meetings were held in glass-walled offices. In this way, Dinesh was central in modernising the travel industry and taking it to the efficient level it is today, a million miles away from the earlier manual systems. Tall, elegantly suited Dinesh, with his impeccable command of the English language, is a far cry from the dress-down look that is associated with the dotcom revolution.

Dinesh encountered a lot of opposition and was teased by friends who wondered why anyone would want to buy using an anonymous computer when they could pick up a phone or call into a shop and enjoy a personal touch. Dinesh did have a few pangs of doubt, at first, because the system worked but bookings were modest. 'Very few people were familiar with the internet at that time, and far less to shop on,' he explains. His misgivings soon eroded and, in 1998, bookings were strong. By September they had achieved 1000 passengers in a month, and Dinesh realised that he was onto something.

October 1998 proved to be a turning point, the beginning of what was to become a global dream. 'I knew the business had to go to the next level', Dinesh says. He had been trying unsuccessfully to raise funding, and in the last six months had made little headway. Suddenly, he recalls, 'I got a call from Jupiter, a US online research company.' Executives at Jupiter had heard about his business and wanted him to speak at a conference in London. The internet was growing in the US and Dinesh sensed the boom was about to come to Europe.

His speech at the conference was well received and Dinesh was approached by some venture capitalists who wanted to invest in the company. Dinesh knew instinctively that he had to get organized fast to take advantage of this opportunity. He needed a concrete business plan and he knew just the person who could help. 'I called up a business associate, Sanjiv Talwar,' Dinesh explains, 'he is a practicing chartered accountant and I needed a finance man. We started writing a business plan, one of many.' He sighs. Finally, on New Year's Day 1999, Dinesh became the chief executive of ebookers.com. Sanjiv, too, sensed the potential of the new company and three months later he joined Dinesh. No plush offices: in the early days, the two men used either end of a single desk. From March they started the serious business of fundraising, but it soon became clear that this wasn't going to be easy in London. Dinesh recalls, 'I spent six months trying to make some headway in London and I got nowhere; within 24 hours of being in the US I got my finance!'

Trying to raise money in London had proved difficult. Dinesh first approached the City firm Arthur Anderson who valued his company at a mere £15 million. Annoyed, Dinesh then went to a major airline and was given even worse news: 'They valued the whole business, including Flightbookers, at just £1.5m and offered to buy half.' Dinesh was not happy.

American Dreams

Undeterred and resolute, Dinesh was confident of the potential growth of his company and, not one to give up easily, he went to New York. The results were instant - within 24 hours, not only did he get his finance but the valuation was good too. The contrast could not have been greater. 'I met some friends for dinner', he recalls. 'I knew it would go well.' On the spot he got an offer of $5 million of funding on a valuation of $55 million. 'They understand business in America,' Dinesh acknowledges. The next day Dinesh was introduced to J P Morgan who saw clear potential in the company. 'They could see the opportunity for ebookers.com in Europe,' Dinesh recalls. 'They were very keen to get into the internet space and they believed in me.' This was the break Dinesh needed and J P Morgan offered to take ebookers.com public on the NASDAQ and Germany's Neuer Market. If he had got the technology from Germany, it was to be America that set the scale for his business.

Dinesh recalls the episode clearly: 'It sounds easy when you say, "we were taken public" but anyone who has ever gone public knows that it's one of those once in a lifetime business experiences that you'll never want to repeat.' It was not easy conducting business in this league and required all his wit and resources. 'We produced business plan after business plan, SEC filings, presentation training, bankers and lawyers...' He sighs when he mentions the lawyers. 'My lawyers, the bank's lawyers, ebookers' lawyers. So many lawyers, I lost count!' The operation required a lot of stamina, particularly the investor road show before the Initial Public Offering (IPO). 'It was like nothing else,' remembers Dinesh. He had no idea what he had let himself in for. He recalls with excitement how 'in the US we had our own Gulf Stream jet'. It was just as well. 'We visited 8 countries in 12 days and we had 72 meetings giving the same presentation without a break!'

Finally, on November 11, 1999, after months of preparation, ebookers.com went public on the NASDAQ in New York and the Neuer Market in Germany. This was the height of the internet boom. The shares floated at $18, raising $61 million. The market capitalisation was $306 million. Soon shares had climbed to $43, giving ebookers.com a valuation of $700 million.

A Successful Formula

So, share prices went through the roof. Dinesh admits, 'Success is scary', and achieving such phenomenal success was a lot to take in. Dinesh did not take his finger off the pulse, however; no champagne parties for him. He realized that, with his rapidly expanding operation and staff base, he had work to do. Not one to waste money, and clear about his responsibilities, he set out to use the new funds to build a business that would one day bring a real return to investors. His employees, now growing in number, were busy in new offices near Russell Square. They were in full swing building websites and designing marketing campaigns. Meanwhile, Dinesh focused his attentions on acquiring companies in order to achieve his vision of making ebookers.com a truly pan-European company. His experience with Royal Nepal of working across 12 EU countries paid off. He bought 11 companies in 7 months and ebookers.com went on to become one of Europe's biggest entrepreneurial success stories.

While many online businesses came and went, Dinesh argues that travel is especially suited to the web. 'Gambling, pornography and travel work online,' he declares. These were the first wave of internet enterprises that really took off. Today companies such as ebay, Google and Facebook have enjoyed enormous success and are part of the second wave of the internet revolution, also known as Web 2.0. Dinesh feels he was in a strong position with ebookers.com. 'We had agreements in place with the airlines, hotels and car-hire companies,' he explains. These links had taken years to build up and so they were well placed to stay ahead of their rivals. It's rare for travel agents to deal with airlines directly to get seats; they tend to go through middlemen like the general sales agents contracted by the airlines. In order to get the best deals, travel companies need to convince individual airlines and hotel chains to let them have contracts. 'It's priceless. These relationships should not be underestimated', Dinesh cautions, 'my first contract with Malaysian Airlines took me four years to get.' He was persistent, 'You just have to keep knocking on doors. Getting a contract with British Airways took me 15 years but it was worth it!' The contract enables you to negotiate access to cheaper fares or, 'distressed inventory', as Dinesh calls it 'These discounts and special offers allow agencies to undercut rivals and are crucial. They are your unique selling point.' He sums this up simply: 'Essentially we knew how to make a profit. We had learnt never to spend more than we earned. Most internet companies didn't do that'.

Business is a continuous learning experience for Dinesh. He has learnt valuable lessons from the start of his entrepreneurial journey which have remained with him ever since. The first was where to focus the business and his strategy always remained clear. 'There were huge price wars with the likes of Thomson and Airtours in the 1980s,' Dinesh recalls, 'they were bidding down prices to a ridiculous level, you could get a week with all meals in Spain including flights for £25. Travel agents made 10 percent of this. That's just £2.50 for selling a holiday. Who can survive on this?' So Dinesh focused the business on the more lucrative mid- to long-haul markets which enjoyed higher margins and bigger-spending customers. Travel to Australia and the Far East, and America too, proved fruitful. 'The no-frills airlines have cornered the short-haul routes in Europe. They're no threat to us, our business complements theirs and actually benefits from it,' asserts Dinesh.

Dinesh stuck to his strategy. He reasons, 'Easyjet and Ryanair, for example, did not need agents, they are direct and simple to use.' These companies had cut out agents and were routing bookings through their own websites and operations. The real business was in the longer flights where there were many more legs in the journey and so agents are of greater value to the consumer. He explains why he took the high road, 'If you are going to Sydney, for example, you may have to go via Singapore. It's difficult for one airline to do all the legs. Airlines could not talk to each other and come to one price for the customer; we could.' He wanted to concentrate on customers who were planning ahead for longer trips. Put simply, 'there was less competition from suppliers and in business it's smart to move to a position where there is less competition.' Furthermore, with their 'cash rich, time poor' clients, they could earn more. As a result, the majority of ebookers' sales are mid- to long-haul flights and he does not see this trend changing: 'People will always travel. We're selling a dream.' He is less enthusiastic about travel for himself, having done it for so many years.

Internet Craze

While getting down to business, people at ebookers.com were not immune to the fact that Europe was going internet crazy. This was an exhilarating time: 'People were lending money to anyone and everyone.' It was a crazy time but an enjoyable one, Dinesh recalls: 'I used to get applications from people who wanted to work in ebookers.com'. It seems people couldn't get enough of the new dotcom companies. 'We had the glamour of the new wave of technology and were riding the crest of it.' This made it a very exciting time to do business and Dinesh feels '...privileged to have experienced being in business at the time of the internet bubble.' He recounts the excitement, the buzz, the energy. 'The market ruled, we were just part of the ocean, the waves carried us up. When the share prices were rising rapidly, many of my IT employees would work all night, and sleep next to their computers. The euphoria was intoxicating. Money is a driver!' He grins and adds, 'when the bubble burst they would clock off at 5.30 p.m. promptly!'

They were learning fast, there was an infectious air and a real energy all around. The world was theirs to conquer and the rising booking figures only added to this feeling. These were heady times. Thankfully Dinesh kept his head and, despite the hysteria around him, did not succumb to wasting money. The papers were full of stories of the amount of money being spent lavishly on parties, perks and crazy deals, but ebookers.com avoided any spending sprees, which was just as well - the other parties were short lived.

The Bubble Bursts

By May 2000 the game ended and they were to face the devastation of the bubble bursting. 'Our value fell from US $770 million to US $30 million virtually overnight', recalls a shaken Dinesh. 'We were in shock.' Share prices plummeted and it was the end of many internet companies. The champagne parties had ground to a halt and offices were suddenly left empty. Ebookers.com survived, but only just.

The internet crash could not have come at a worse time. Ebookers.com was due to go back for secondary fundraising in July, to take the company to profitability. The market was against them. The media did not help either with its sensational dotcom 'death lists'. The companies that they had boosted in the press a few months ago were suddenly vilified. People lost faith in the value of internet companies and ebookers.com's share price fell to just $6. This was devastating. Dinesh was really frustrated; he had a company that worked, they had met all their business obligations to date and he knew they could continue to do so. He had total confidence in the company; the problem lay in convincing others.

Dinesh resorted to putting in $3 million of his personal money to demonstrate his belief in the company. They also, crucially, had a healthy set of half year financial results. Undeterred and full of new-found vigour, Dinesh visited some of his major European shareholders. He managed to raise $45 million and thus secured the future of the business and his staff. He could sleep easy.

He remained cautious, however. Cost conscious at the best of times, he tightened the corporate belt even more. The company cut their costs to the core. The strategy worked and they put out better and better figures, proving the City wrong. 'What saved us,' explains Dinesh 'is that we didn't build a business around a website but a website around a business.' Ebookers was still making 30 percent of its sales through shops and call centres. Dinesh was hugely relieved when the slide stopped and, having saved the company and secured its future, he could concentrate on the day-to-day business. However, another disaster was about to occur at a scale he could not possibly have imagined.

September 11

It was a time of rapid recovery for the company. They had their highest ever online bookings in the first week of September 2001. Things generally were picking up and going well, and outside scepticism waned. Then, out of nowhere, disaster struck. No one could have predicted the 9/11 tragedy and the chaos it would cause. The travel industry worldwide was in disarray. Dinesh was watching CNN in his office when the first plane hit the Twin Towers. 'I had no idea the extent of the tragedy or the impact it would have on my business,' he says. As events unfolded, he was inundated with customers calling to cancel their trips and survival was all he could think of. Drastic measures had to be put in place if they were to make it.

Dinesh kept a cool head and drew from his years of experience in the industry. 'I have been through disasters before and survived,' he states proudly. The Gulf War, the Oklahoma bombing and other tragedies had taken place and eventually people had resumed their travel. He knew this would happen again. His philosophy was to cut back and wait for recovery. They had to reduce their spending even further and tighten their belts. 'I know the consumer,' Dinesh claims, 'I knew they will always travel whether for pleasure or business.' He had good insights and a lot of inner reserve to ride the storm. He was convinced the industry would recover and that ebookers.com would ride the crest of the wave once more.

When the Going Gets Tough...

'We had to make redundancies; it was difficult and depressing for everyone', recalls Dinesh sadly. Even though he was faced with this tough task, he tried to minimize the redundancies and indeed later went on to create even more employment than at his earlier peak. This was a difficult time for him, but his survival instincts kicked in and he remained upbeat. His optimism was realised and ebookers rose out of the ashes stronger than before. It was growing at a faster pace, powered by the growing popularity of the internet, and they were ahead of their rivals. But Dinesh had learnt from September 11: 'I learnt then that we had to always be prepared and be lean and nimble as a business the whole time.' He set about giving ebookers.com the lowest and most flexible cost structure in the industry.

A year after 9/11, the 'bricks and mortar' travel industry was still bruised while ebookers.com enjoyed rapid growth. The travel industry is not for the faint hearted. When Al Gore, former US Vice President, said, 'We are ready for any unforeseen event which may or may not occur,' he could have been referring to the travel industry. Having just got over 9/11, they were faced with SARS and the outbreak of the Iraq war. The past few years have been some of the most tumultuous the travel world has ever known.

But not only did ebookers.com survive, it thrived. Dinesh went on to acquire Travelbag holdings in February 2003, which was another leading UK travel company. The 9/11 situation not only effected them deeply as a company but also unwittingly took them to India. They had been planning to outsource to India, as was then the trend, in order to reduce costs.

Dinesh, like many Asian entrepreneurs, also turned to the 'global village'. Being of Indian origin, he was well placed to utilize his contacts and networks in India. He saw its potential and once again, looked to the US for signals. He found that half the Fortune 500 companies out-sourced some functions to India. It would suit their business needs too; India was the centre for IT and academic excellence. They had high-quality graduates ready and eager to work. In addition, local salaries were a fraction of what it would cost to pay them in the west.

The expansion of ebookers.com and its internationalization was not without challenge. Its operations in India were an important part of this success story with 1000 staff employed at the company's main call centre from a total of 2000 around the globe. Many of the workers sent to work in the Indian call centres were from Finland and spoke Finnish, one of the world's rarest languages. Dinesh took an entrepre-neurial stance in filling the posts: 'We offered Finnish graduates trips to India, with free flights and accommodation, to work for local rates of pay at the call centre for a year.' He had clearly hit on a successful formula because the prospect of an Indian working holiday drew 150 applications for five places: 'We had people from Sweden, Norway, Switzerland, France, Germany and Denmark.'

Ebookers.com had been thinking of outsourcing to India to reduce costs. 'We had seen the General Electric complex near New Delhi, which had 5000 people,' Dinesh says. Then 9/11 happened and they had to act: 'We went full tilt to India to reduce costs'. Ebookers even-tually operated a Business Process Outsourcing facility in New Delhi. There, a graduate workforce carried out business processes for the ebookers.com group, including customer service and email sales. Ebookers.com's India operation - known as Tecnovate - started on a relatively small scale but then grew to employ 1000 staff. This facility has been critical to both the growth and the profitability of the European businesses. Not only did the operations in India enable the company to cut costs but the increase in efficiency was tremendous. India was also five hours ahead of the UK so the average 600 to 700 tickets sold per day were ready for processing by the time the UK staff arrived in their offices at 9 a.m. It turned the operation into a 24-hour one rather than one limited to the traditional working day. It's a cut-throat, competitive world and Dinesh was constantly looking for innovative ways to reduce costs and raise quality. After a series of world disasters, he was constantly wary. Ever innovative, they soon opened the Business Process Outsourcing to third-party clients, thus generating a new income stream and benefiting from economies of scale. Dinesh had found a way to turn a cost centre into a profit centre. So, from the giddy heights of success to doom and despair, he survived where many failed. This accomplished entrepreneur made his mark in the tough world of travel, and showed his grit during the most devastating global events.

Serial Entrepreneur

Dinesh Dhamija sold ebookers.com in 2005 to US-based travel group Cedant in an all-cash deal close to $500 million. Cedant, one of the world's largest travel groups, also owns Avis and Budget car rental groups and Galileo. Dinesh stayed as a consultant to the company for nine months in 2005.

After a brief stint in India dabbling with property and private equity, Dinesh has now set his sights on property development in Romania with his new company Copper Beech, inspired by the trees which take 150 years to grow. His brother-in-law was the Indian Ambassador there, and he was introduced to the country in March 2005. His brother-in-law left in July, but Dinesh had by then established a few good contacts. In June 2006 he made his first investment in Bucharest. Since then the Copper Beech group has bought 1500 acres of land in and around the capital. Romania joined the EU in January 2007 and foreign investment there has now gone through the roof. This happened when Ireland joined the EU, sending property prices sky high, and Copper Beech is enjoying the same trend in Romania. It is going to build 16,600 residential dwellings on this land in 17 different projects. 'Our first project of 156 apartments was launched in September 2007 and 80 percent sold within just two days!' Dinesh says proudly. 'We are now the largest residential property development company in Romania.'

Dinesh started his entrepreneurial journey by trying to avoid paying the excessive tax he was having deducted from his pay packet every month. Coming full circle and being entrepreneurially creative, Dinesh declares that one of the benefits of being a non-domiciled resident and a world traveller is that you can find tax havens. He has got the formula right, it seems. Still in his fifties, Dinesh Dhamija has undoubtedly been a huge player in the UK Asian business success story. His story illustrates innovation, courage and creativity. His strength in business lies in thinking laterally and looking at the bigger picture; he spots trends and learns from events in different countries. A pioneer of the IT revolution, he created the landmark ebookers.com, and became a business role model to be proud of. The travel industry has endured nightmare trading conditions over recent years but Dinesh says, 'We knew we'd survive. The question was whether we would become number one or number two in Europe.'

Background Reading

Adams, R., 'All the fun of the fare: interview with Dinesh Dhamija, chief executive, ebookers', *Guardian*, Aug. 31, 2002.

NRI Internet.com, London, Ebookers: http://www.nriinternet.com, Dec 3, 2004.

Time, Inc., 'E-bookers: Dinesh Dhamija', *Time Magazine*, Oct. 27, 2003.

Firoz Kassam

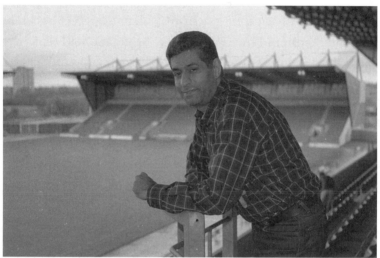

Reproduced by permission of Firoz Kassam

Firoz Kassam is one of the most dynamic and energetic of our entrepreneurs who goes from strength to strength. Kassam's tale has all the charm of a rags to riches story but offers much more. If this story was a novel it could well be one of the 'ripping yarns' of Charles Dickens or even a Jeffrey Archer page-turner; it is a tale of business success and of hubris almost causing a downfall before redemption and recovery. It is a tale of adaptation and assimilation into a new country and the exploitation of a controversial niche market. Firoz Kassam's journey has taken him from fish and chips to football. When he came to the UK he washed dishes in a take-away shop, later owned one and then got into the hotel trade. He couldn't find tourists to fill his hotels, so he put up the homeless and asylum seekers and was paid by the government for doing this. Today, the Firoka Group of Companies consists of several hotels, including the flagship Holiday Inn in King's Cross, Holiday Inn Expresses in the City and Oxford, as well as a Sheraton Hotel in Vancouver. Firoz Kassam now has interests including golf clubs, conference centres, restaurants and leisure parks. He has a 500-acre Oxfordshire estate and a castle in Warwickshire. He is better known as the former Chairman of Oxford United Football Club, which he brought back from the brink of bankruptcy; he then built the Kassam Stadium. Firoz Kassam has been, and will remain, one to watch. Still in his fifties, he is worth an estimated £275 million.

Chapter 5

African Adventures

Firoz Kassam was born into poverty in Tanzania, East Africa in the 1950s. He was one of five children with only their father's small confectionery business to support them. His life of hardship took a turn for the worse when his mother died while he was still a child and he had to share responsibility for his younger brothers and sisters. In this difficult environment, Kassam and his family were able to come out with that most precious of gifts: an education. This Kassam credits to his mother – 'she was our inspiration, our needs always came first' – and one of the tragedies of this tale is that she died without seeing the success of her eldest child: 'One of my biggest regrets is that she didn't live long enough to see what we have built. It is a testament to her.' Further sadness was to follow. The death of an elder brother led Firoz to quit school early and to sacrifice his education to help run the family business so his siblings could finish theirs. This was a noble gesture for the young Kassam to make.

He and his family were part of the large Indian community in East Africa. During the time, when large parts of India were occupied by the British Empire, Indians were encouraged to migrate to Africa to form an 'educated middle class' of shopkeepers, engineers and doctors. By the late 1960s, many newly independent African countries had begun to resent the fact that their commercial economies were dominated by Indians. Some countries, like Uganda, expelled their Indian residents forcing them to abandon their successful businesses and leave the country. The 70s saw an exodus of East African Asians and Firoz Kassam was one of many who came to Britain.

Streets Paved with Gold

Kassam was only 19 years old when he left to seek his fortune in Britain. It was a bold move and what was to be the start of an eventful journey in the UK: 'I left my family and came out here to really see what the West had to offer.' The family were behind him but his trip was not entirely smooth. He encountered problems with immigration officials on arrival. 'They wouldn't let me in!' he laughs. 'They would only give me a short-term visa.' However, because his parents were British subjects from India and Kassam had not renounced his nationality he made his application at the first opportunity and was relieved: 'I was told I was entitled to a British passport.'

Like many Asians he headed for the bright lights of London where the streets were meant to be paved with gold. Young, ambitious and full of curiosity and optimism, he had the bravado of youth. Whether he knew then that he would make his millions many times over in this country is not known, for the early days here were far humbler. 'My first job was washing dishes in an Indian takeaway shop,' he reminisces. 'That was where it all started'. Small beginnings, maybe, but from this start Kassam was to build a property empire as he started building hotels in the style of a real-life Monopoly player.

Brixton – and Beginnings

Britain in the 70s was no picnic for any immigrant community and in places like Brixton things were probably worst than most. It was to crime-ridden Brixton that Kassam decamped in 1978, into a hotbed of social unrest, deprivation and exclusion. Kassam was to have a front-row seat as Brixton became the frontline of riots and civil unrest.

Kassam rented the Fisherman's Net, a fish and chip shop, and this was to be his first business venture in Britain. He had to work very hard and the trade was normally at night. In those days Brixton was dangerous; it was a run down area and Kassam had a ring-side view of the riots which broke out. The allure of fish and chips soon faded and his next step was to rent a property in Olympia.

Kassam was married by now and he and his wife lived in a flat in the property. 'We cleaned up the place and turned it into a bed and breakfast,' he says. The Olympia Bed and Breakfast had 20 rooms and cost Kassam £25,000 a year in rent. The payments were difficult to keep up and the time came when Kassam couldn't afford to continue to pay that rent and carry on surviving. This was a turning point in his business life. 'I got involved in a "niche" market,' he explains.

There was an enormous demand to cater for the homeless at that time and Kassam had vacant rooms. It all made perfect sense to him: 'I was running a business and what businesses do is identify opportunities in a market or a set of circumstances and create something that allows them to take advantage of it.' Renting out properties to local authorities who paid a premium to house homeless people inevitably lead to bad headlines and charges of profiteering. Kassam is unrepentant. 'What was I supposed to do? Keep the rooms empty and keep the homeless on the street? Sure, I made a lot of money but I also helped a lot of people find a warm room and a roof over their heads,' he says. Whatever the ethics, he prospered and profited from taking in the homeless. His fortune swelled from six to seven figures.

This set the foundation for his property empire and formed the Firoka Group. By the mid 80s he had several properties in the Victoria area of London. It had taken him 10 years of blood, sweat and tears to build a property portfolio of 20 properties covering an entire square in Victoria. His vision was to convert them into a 400-room hotel. But having acquired all the properties and obtained planning permission, the rug was pulled from under his feet. Britain hit a recession in the early 90s and the bankers repossessed his properties. His early success and overextension led to disaster; he had been overconfident and borrowed too much. It was a bitter blow. He lost almost everything he had and barely managed to keep a roof over his own head.

How does a man who seemed to have it all recover from such a blow? Running a growing empire one day and having the rug pulled the next? Kassam explains: 'Faith really matters to me, my belief in God, in Allah, is what pulled us through. I am proud to be a Muslim and proud to attend my local mosque five evenings a week whenever I can'.

A Glimmer of Hope

Some would call it luck and others would say it was judgement, but what allowed the business to ride the storm was that the banks granted him permission to carry on building the Holiday Inn in King's Cross. It was no vacation, but the Holiday Inn helped him carry on, albeit with much lower margins than he was used to or which were ideal. He clawed his way out of the financial difficulties by resorting to a tried and tested money-spinner. He bought the London Park Hotel in 1992 in the Elephant and Castle, south London – another socially deprived area. This hotel was catering for the budget end of the tourist market when he bought it. He continued providing cheap rooms for tourists for a couple of years but did not see any real returns. He then spotted a niche market for asylum seekers and the homeless. This was far more lucrative.

Since then Kassam has worked his way to a multimillion-pound fortune. He has built a hotel, property and leisure empire and made his mark on UK plc. Kassam puts it down to being lucky and being in the right place at the right time, and adds, 'It's not something I ever dreamt of. Never. It is by God's grace.' It's much more than fate, though; Kassam has a sharp intellect and business acumen.

So how does Kassam manage to successfully run a business employing hundreds of people? The answer is that he surrounds himself with a small group of select people whom he trusts to make the kind of decisions he would approve of. He is a challenging boss and his strength is that he really knows what the business needs: 'I start at the end with the vision of what we need to deliver and from that we work out the deals we need to pull to achieve that.' This probably means that Kassam is not really a details man, he is not driven by the day-to-day nuts and bolts of running the business. Like a modern-day Gordon Gekko or a reincarnation of Lords Hanson and White, he is driven by the deal; business gets boring without day to day challenges. Like any entrepreneur, it's the creativity, the innovation, the drive that matter to him.

Be Careful What You Wish for – Football Fiasco

Kassam was restless. Still only in his forties, his business was in order, his hotels and property portfolio were strong and he was bored. He wanted to get his teeth into something new and exciting. His wish was to be granted. An ailing football club was in need of a new owner.

Oxford is a place of contrasts. At one extreme are the dreamy spires of the university which have, for hundreds of years, inspired and motivated generations of undergraduates and rewarded intellectual excellence with Nobel prizes and a global reputation. At the other end is the city's football team, Oxford United. The initials may be the same but that's about it. Fleeting success under the late Robert Maxwell was a distant memory when Kassam appeared on the scene and bought the company for just £1. Football is littered with stories of the bargain which came good or the underdog who defied the odds, but Kassam and Oxford United is not one of those stories. He may have bought the club for £1 but he was soon to realize just what an expensive £1 it would turn out to be.

For that investment Kassam got a failing team, a home ground in such a state of disrepair that health and safety requirements meant the team was not allowed to play there, and a new stadium that was just half finished and had been badly designed without the slightest consideration as to how it would be built or even how it would be funded.

These things on their own were bad but what made it worse was the debt the club was in, all £18 million of it. There is a fine line between bravery and stupidity, between a challenge and a leap too far. Had Kassam bitten off more than he could chew? Was he a novice playing in the majors? Whatever the case, these were the conditions Kassam inherited. Was it just the challenge he needed?

The circumstances of the final match Oxford United played at the old Manor Ground were stark. They were in the first division, now the Championship, on the verge of relegation to the second division. Penniless, their future was uncertain and it could easily have been their last game. The fans turned to Kassam to save them. 'When we move to the new ground, I will deliver on what I promised,' he said. The fans would learn that he is a man of integrity and his word is his bond.

Kassam was the saviour the club needed even though he had arrived at the eleventh hour; it needed a businessman to save the day. The plan was to start the rebuilding programme again with a view to building other income-generating activities around the stadium to support the club in the longer term. 'I needed a challenge so I thought, great, I'll take it on,' says Kassam ruefully. He was Britain's first Asian Chairman of a professional football club. However, his visions of finishing the half-built stadium and developing a site at the new Minchery Farm location hit a brick wall. City planners and local businesses were opposed, and when he decided to name the stadium 'Kassam Stadium' after himself it raised questions about his motives.

The football world resented this businessman whom they felt was not a serious football man. He was met with suspicion and cynicism from the outset. Some football pundits were very anti-Kassam; the fans, on the other hand, were undecided. They were delighted that their club was going to be saved and thought that Kassam's naming the stadium after himself showed his commitment to the club and the town, but the jury was still out. There was a feeling that the support activities were more important in generating money for Kassam. It remained to be seen just how concrete his commitment was. 'You don't go into football to make money despite what every fan in every pub up and down the country may think,' says Kassam. 'I had to run that fine line – I didn't want to make money out of Oxford but I couldn't pump money into the club day after day, week after week, year after year. The fans can scream and shout but my pockets are not bottomless pits.' That was not a position he could sustain, nor should any self-respecting business person. Whatever his motivations, he saved the club.

He found the professional football arena far tougher than running hotels. For a private man, Kassam was to find the football world relentless. He was a tough negotiator and an excellent dealmaker, but the football world was outside his comfort zone. Ex-Tory MP David Mellor was a big critic who described Kassam as not being the 'ideal knight on a white charger' but simply a property developer. This was all a little bit easy coming from a man who resigned in disgrace as a minister, who then lost his seat in the 1997 election and who swapped a lifetime of commitment to Fulham when Russian billions arrived at Chelsea. 'It was my money, millions of it, going into Oxford United,' says Kassam, 'my effort, my time, my energy', and he simply didn't have time to waste attending to the opinions of those on the sidelines who had never taken the same risks, made the same investments or the same long term commitment. Legal proceedings were not followed against Mellor; it really wasn't worth it – after all Kassam had a club to run, not a club to just write about.

Race Against Time

The new season would be crucial. Kassam had three months to deliver the new stadium, hire a new manager and new players to live up to his promises to the fans, and to confound his critics. The criticism he faced was relentless; he had many vocal critics. They implied he was not really a 'football person'. As Jimmy Greaves said, 'this football is a silly old game'. Previous football people had got Oxford into a mess and the only solution was a calm-headed, rational, business approach, not overemotional talk and hot-headed fans.

The character assassination campaign was debilitating. Kassam is tall and smart, soft spoken and amiable, though under pressure he can be ruthless. He is shy and often masks his insecurity which is often misunderstood as arrogance. He is an extremely sensitive man and the barbs cut him deep. The whole episode took a toll on his health and family life. Did the fans realise the extent of the damage they were doing to the one man who was pumping in his own money to rescue their club? Kassam was overwhelmed; had he bitten off more than he could chew? The world of football was strange and one maybe Kassam didn't want membership of, but he was trapped. A man of his word and great business integrity, he had to deliver. He had put so much of his time and money into this very public project only to be treated like a villain rather than a hero.

Kassam was frustrated at being misunderstood, confused as to whether it was mandatory to give everything up to love the game or actually make it a sustainable venture. He was disparaged because he was not married to football. The way things were at this point, he had everything going against him and he would need to work miracles to deliver.

Legal bills easily ran into six figures. Twenty-four months of hard work and misery. Was it all worth it? Kassam is emotional about this; he talks about it 'breaking my spirit and breaking my heart'. Perhaps it was worth it. Ten months after the turn of the new millennium, Kassam was finally able to announce that work on the new stadium could finally restart. The beginning of the end? The end of the beginning? Time, that unflinching and unstoppable force, would be the judge.

Lord of the Manor

Not one to be down and out for long and always looking for an opportunity, Kassam was to take his next leap in the property market. When the nearby Heythrop Park Estate, set in 500 acres of parkland, went up for sale he snapped it up as his home for a cool £15 million. He fell in love with it as soon as he saw the gardens; one look and he was set. Heythrop Park had been too big as a training centre for its former owners NatWest, and it was too big a home for Kassam. He did what he does best; he used his business acumen and turned it into a five-star hotel. The football, meanwhile, had not gone away.

Tension Mounts

So, would Kassam deliver? Would the stadium be finished in time for the first game? Would this be a challenge he could enjoy? Kassam is adamant that, 'there is no real joy in football, just nerves. If we lose the fans get to walk away and drown their sorrows but as Chairman there is an awful lot riding on whether we do something as simple as scoring more goals than the opposition. The 90 minutes on the pitch are the worst, my heart is always in my mouth. There is so, so much depending on it.' The situation was fraught and tempers were running high. It was a close call. Kassam was ruthless under pressure. He wanted results.

In two years Kassam sacked four managers, claiming they didn't perform. His fifth manager was Mark Wright, the former Liverpool Captain and England player. A few more managers came and went after Mark Wright, but still no success on the pitch for Oxford United – although they did come close.

Running a business is a challenge in itself. Running a property and hotel business the size of Kassam's would make a weaker man crumble. Running that business and then running a football club on top is a challenge on a whole new level. For a man who ran on adrenaline, where the next deal had to be more exciting than the previous one, it is always easy to lose sight of the things that matter. 'I think I may have lost a little perspective. Sure, the business really mattered, as did the football club,' Kassam says, 'but I should have taken better care of myself. The heart troubles were a big wake-up sign, it made me look at my life in a whole new way.' He now had to make some tough personal and professional decisions. So what did he do, this man who had lived his life – private, professional and sporting – at breakneck speed? How did he manage to let go and get some of that work life balance back? No half measures; he knew he had to make major changes and put some distance between himself and the difficulties of his past. The best decision at that time was to pack his bags and relocate to Monaco, still commuting once or twice a week to keep on top of the businesses.

Back to the Game

All was still not well back at the ranch. With only days to go before the first 'friendly' game at their stadium, Oxford United had still not been given the go-ahead by officials; safety approval was still pending. Precisely 24 hours before the match was to start the officials, ambulance, police and council descended on the ground. It was an anxious time. So much was riding on their approval and the thought of disappointing the fans at this stage was more than Kassam could bear. He didn't need to worry; the safety certificate was awarded, albeit with conditions attached. The game could go ahead but with 2000 spectators below full capacity. It was a close call.

August 4, 2001 was a historic day for Oxford United. They finally played in the pristine £15 million stadium for the first time. Kassam was now a household name in Oxford and it was his biggest day since he had set foot in Britain. The match was Oxford United versus Crystal Palace, and Oxford won with a penalty shoot-out. The roar from the crowds was deafening and Kassam was elated. They had christened the new stadium with their first victory. Kassam had delivered.

Making a Fortune – Perspectives from Firoz Kassam

Kassam is a great believer in the maxim 'if opportunity knocks then open the door'. He founded his empire and fortune on spotting the needs in the economy and accommodating these. He realised that his budget hotels could be more usefully employed housing asylum seekers and homeless families. This was high on the government agenda and he was not about to look a gift horse in the mouth. The local authorities were prepared to pay premium prices for his rooms and that meant he was running his properties at full capacity. 'Where do you think the cash came from to build this business?' he asks. 'From those deals with the local authorities. I found a niche market, I developed it and, yes, I made profit out of it. By doing that, the government benefited and did something about the homeless; the homeless benefited as they had somewhere to live and now hundreds of people have jobs in the business that it built.'

It is easy to remember only the good times. When we look back we remember the summer days when it did not rain or the times when our team won and didn't lose. But we learn best when we look back and think about the failures, the disasters. Learning happens when things don't go to plan. What has Kassam learnt from the bad old days and the property fiasco in Victoria? 'Borrowing money is the easy option, paying the money back is the hard part,' he says wistfully. Kassam recalls the period in all its awful glory: overexpansion and overconfidence, everything on the block including his home and personal guarantees. Kassam is self-aware, he knows he made mistakes but also blames the banks: 'they cut and run too quickly. I'm an entrepreneur, I make deals and take risks and so there will be good and bad times. I know it but I'm not sure the banks do.'

Nowadays it is all different, cash has become cheap to Kassam and he has banks lining up to lend him money. But has he learnt? You bet. 'What I do now, I do with my money and no one else's. See these grey hairs? Every single one of them has been bought and paid for over the

past few years in good and bad times. But they're my grey hairs and I'll
not pass them onto the banks by borrowing money when I don't need
to.' For Kassam the reward is not only in doing what he does but also
in achieving it with his own resources.

Any advice from Kassam? 'Sure, you can learn lessons from what I've
done,' he says, 'and the biggest lessons of all is don't buy a football
club!' What was it that bought a sober man of faith into the business
of the nation's favourite game? 'It was a moment of pure madness,' he
says. To the outsider, the fans and the commentators it looks a sexy
business; which football fan, after all, has not dreamt of owning his
own team? 'Be careful what you wish for,' says a reflective Kassam.
'The game and business looks so different depending on where you're
sitting. Trust me, the view from the director's box is very different to
the view from the terraces.'

Football is not only a funny old game, it is also a cruel one. Invest in
a football club and you are often investing in someone else's dream
and shattered dreams make for broken hearts and bitter recrimina-
tions. Were Kassam's heart problems a result of the non-stop abuse,
the endless onslaught and a daily barrage of criticism? No one knows
for sure, but there must be a link. 'The fans were behind me at first,'
Kassam remembers. 'I had saved their club. But, after a while, dealing
with planning authorities and fans took their toll. My big lesson. If
you don't like being criticized in the most personal and hurtful terms,
find a new business because you really don't want to be in football.'

The problem with football is that no one is ever satisfied. As one season ends, planning for the next season begins and the next year has
always got to be better than the last one. Next year the fans will want
more wins, more points and the chairman to invest more of his
money because, to the fans, the club belongs to them and not to the
people who pay the wages or foot the bills. Kassam had been
successful because he kept his businesses in private hands but for the
fans it didn't matter whose name was on the deeds. 'They buy a season ticket and they think they have bought the club,' reflects Kassam.

'Football shows that the business of football and the romance and passion of football don't always go together.' For Kassam it was not a business, but it was also not a hobby. It was a commitment, but not an open cheque. 'I am as committed as any chairman of any club in the land,' he pointed out, 'but you can't spend money like it has no value. Whatever happens, the club needs to be successful.'

And What Now?

Having saved the club and built the stadium, Kassam sold Oxford United FC for £2 million (and made a small loss) on March 21, 2006 to Oxford man Nick Merry, who lives in the US. Merry has brought back Jim Smith, who was the man who put Oxford United into the first division. The stadium still carries Kassam's name because the club did not have the funds to make the purchase.

Kassam's portfolio continues to grow. He is currently busy refurbishing many of his existing hotels and upgrading his golf clubs from 9 to 18 holes. He has a Holiday Inn in King's Cross, and two Holiday Inn Express hotels, one in London City, the other at the Kassam Stadium in Oxford. He owns Studley Castle in Warwickshire as well as Heythrop Park in Oxford and a hotel in Canada. For the past couple of years he has been working on acquiring Alexandra Palace in London, which he has now taken over. He is concentrating on what he is best at, the hotel and property empire. His dalliance with the football world has left scars. In a world where there is no certainty, where any decision can lead to good or bad outcomes, this man was not afraid to take on a challenge and see it through no matter what the cost. And the cost has been dear for both his health and his family. He remains a devoted father to his children. Whatever happens next, Kassam is set to stay in the limelight.

Background Reading

BBC 2, *Bindi Millionaires: Rags to Riches*, 'Firoz Kassam', BBC Birmingham, 2000

Dr Kartar Lalvani

Photo supplied by Kartar Lalvani

The brand name Vitabiotics is better known than its owner, Kartar Lalvani, who founded Britain's first specialist vitamin supplement company in 1971. Kartar Lalvani came to Britain from India in 1956 and, after completing a postgraduate degree in Pharmacy at King's College, went to Bonn University where he obtained a doctorate in Medicinal Chemistry with distinction. He has since become a fellow of the Royal Pharmaceutical Society. After working in pharmamedical research for several years and gaining some valuable patents, he founded Vitabiotics. This has become a leading brand with national and international distribution. Kartar has had many accolades heaped upon him: he has been Asian of the Year for the respected

Asian Who's Who and his company received the Queen's Award for enterprise in international trade in May 2003 and a GlaxoSmithKline award for innovation in medical science in 2006. He is now worth in excess of £100 million. The modest and visionary Kartar has ensured that all Vitabiotics products are linked with related charities and has made many contributions to the wider community.

Chapter 6

Neon Signs

As you travel down the North Circular Road in Dollis Hill, north London, you can't miss the Vitabiotics sign. It symbolises the strength of the marketing effort behind one of the UK's fastest-growing brands of well-being products. The firm's marketing hits the nail on the head and, unlike many entrepreneurs, Kartar prefers to stay in the background and let his products speak for themselves. The company commissions research and surveys to launch each new brand and uses these to generate numerous column inches in the national press and glossy magazines. For example, it commissioned research into the attitudes of modern women. 'What women want' screamed the headlines from newspapers and a no-holds barred controversy ensued. The survey, which had been commissioned by Vitabiotics Wellbeing, found that one in five mothers thought that working mothers equalled bad mothers. This hugely sensitive finding caused outrage, resulting in huge headlines and pages of debate for and against the issue. And yet another poll commissioned by Vitabiotics Wellbeing found that nearly one in three women think marriage is no longer necessary. This world-renowned scientist is, therefore, not averse to causing outrageous debate and controversy. His company's surveys cover topics ranging from the menopause to detox to pregnancy.

Remarkable, indeed, if you look at the man behind the scenes. Quiet, shy, and avoiding the limelight, this Sikh who wears his turban with pride seems the least likely person to encourage the starkest of gender debates. Who would imagine that this quiet gentleman could cause so much controversy? The headlines prove otherwise and have certainly launched his products with gusto. Should these be seen as healthy debates on health or controversial and headline-grabbing sales drives? Either way, the formula has worked and Vitabiotics has taken a lead in the already crowded vitamin and health sector.

Critics need to see the whole picture; Kartar's formula is much more complex than simply grabbing headlines and pushing products. Every product is linked to a related charity and Kartar donates generously. For example, taking the lead in educational campaigns, Vitabiotics established the National Menopause Alliance with partner charities in the UK to raise awareness of the health risks faced by women. Kartar elaborates on this giving: 'We fervently believe in our products and it's important for us to support the groups we are targeting.' So the process is clear, you commission research via surveys and polls which will get the public's attention, followed by a successful launch of the product and then donations to a specific related charity. A win-win formula. Sales are healthy and money is given to worthy causes. The success and sustainability of Vitabiotics' products – such as Wellwoman capsules or Perfectil for skin, hair and nails – in a hugely competitive market demonstrates their quality and popularity.

The Man Himself

If you visit Kartar at his London headquarters, you will be struck by how tasteful the reception area is. There are plants and a large Japanese rock feature, illustrating the company ethos of 'nature meets science'. The other thing that you notice as you enter is a sign which says Binatone. This gives a hint of the mark of entrepreneurial success made by this family. Binatone is associated with the flamboyant entrepreneur Gulu Lalvani who has often been linked with beautiful women, the most famous of all being Princess Diana. He happens to be the brother of Kartar and they are clearly close.

Kartar is approachable to the people who work for him and takes an interest in their welfare, particularly regarding health issues. Health is a passion for him, not just a business. The receptionist commented, 'He's a really nice man, we always chat. I told him I wanted more upper body strength and he said he would show me the best way.' He has 70 employees in London alone and they come from a range of cultures and backgrounds. Many have been with him for several years and are loyal to him. They are situated on several floors in open-plan offices and almost everything, other than manufacturing, is kept in-house. Going beyond family businesses in the traditional sense, Kartar sees Vitabiotics as a 'greater family business'. The board room boasts a grand round table in the middle with large, comfortable leather chairs. Photographs and plaques adorn the walls and Vitabiotics products are displayed proudly in glass cabinets. From the windows you can see the new Wembley stadium with its blinking eye.

Shrewd and attentive, compassionate and caring, Kartar is a complex character. This gentle dynamo is passionate about what he does. This goes back to his training as a scientist. His passion is his research, and he has faith in his products. It hasn't been an easy ride. However, he's been in business for over 30 years, and Vitabiotics still has a young, fresh feel to it.

Family Fortunes

Kartar was born in Karachi in 1931 before the India–Pakistan partition. The turmoil of the partition disrupted his schooling and his family were forced to move to Bombay, now Mumbai. Born into a Sikh family, he was the second eldest in a family of eight children (four boys and four girls). They maintain their close relationship even though they are now spread out geographically. All the brothers are enterprising and in business, though not together.

The best known member of the family is the youngest brother Gulu, not only for his penchant for beautiful women, but as owner of

Binatone, one of the world's largest manufacturers of digital cordless phones and one of the largest privately owned consumer electronics companies in the UK. Binatone, named after their youngest sister Bina, was founded in 1958 by Gulu and brother Partap to import radios from Hong Kong. The business has now been divided and both brothers have their own Binatone groups operating in different parts of the world. Another interesting fact about this entrepreneurial family is that Gulu Lalvani was one of the initial founders of Binatone, where Sir Alan Sugar worked in his early years. The family connections boast not just royalty but also society heirs. Gulu's daughter, Divia, is married to chocolate heir Joel Michael Cadbury.

Kartar's other brother is involved in pharmaceuticals in Nigeria. Kartar too has factories in Nigeria, as well as in India, Egypt and Indonesia. They are pharmaceutical factories providing prescription products for the local economics. In the UK the Vitabiotics licence operates in four different factories as well as one in Sweden and one in Switzerland, all specialising in health and well-being products.

You don't have to try to hard too work out where Kartar got his inspiration from. Going back to his childhood, Kartar recalls proudly, 'My father was a pharmacist in Karachi, he was the largest wholesaler in the Sindh area.' These early influences were important and set the scene for his future empire. His father was clearly a strong role model who both encouraged and inspired Kartar. All the Lalvani children had a moderately traditional upbringing in a Sikh household but were encouraged to be forward thinking. Their father guided all his children to be educated and to study hard. Kartar took this to a high level and was particularly scholarly. He is the most highly educated of all his siblings, and passionate about it. The Lalvanis enjoyed a comfortable lifestyle.

However, they were soon to lose everything they had built up in Pakistan during the turbulence of the partition. Like many others, the Lalvani family were under pressure to leave the area they had grown up in. 'We left before the fighting started,' says Kartar. The partition saw millions of people, from both India and Pakistan, torn from their families and displaced during this period. 'If we had not left our lives would be under threat,' Kartar explains, seriously. It was devastating for the young Kartar. 'Many of those who stayed lost their lives,' he reminisces. This was a difficult time. 'We had to start from scratch in Bombay,' Kartar recalls. But, undeterred in the face of tragedy, 'my father made it again in a few years', says Kartar proudly. In Bombay his father started a pharmaceutical factory; it was through its success that he managed to pay for his children to be educated. Kartar would later inherit this resilience.

After graduating in Pharmacy in Ahmedabad in India, Kartar pursued his studies in England where he arrived in 1956. He completed a postgraduate degree in Pharmacy at King's College, London and then went on to Bonn University in Germany in 1959 to embark on a doctorate in Medicinal Chemistry which he gained with distinction in 1962. It was while he was studying in London that he met and was taught by Arnold Beckett, then a lecturer and now a professor, who was later to be the Chair of Vitabiotics. After working for ten years in active pharma-medical research, and gaining some valuable patents, Kartar was to found Vitabiotics, Britain's first specialist vitamin supplement company in 1971.

A Breakthrough

Kartar had always harboured a desire to run his own business, but it was a personal problem that was to unwittingly open the door. He suffered from persistent mouth ulcers and was frustrated that he could not find any effective treatments for the ailment. There was nothing available on the market that worked. Putting his scientist's brain into action, he finally found what he thought was the solution. He tested it on himself and it worked. He called his mouth ulcer treatment Oralcer and it was from this that Vitabiotics was later to be born.

The path to riches is hardly ever smooth and Kartar faced a challenging start as he tried to licence Oralcer to the larger pharmaceuticals
who, he felt, could produce and sell it on to pharmacies and retail outlets far more easily than he could. They already had the manufacturing and sales operations up and running and it would be a fairly
straightforward process for them. Sadly, his logic was not shared by
these large companies, and trying to persuade them to do things his
way was another issue as they didn't see the potential for his product.
Kartar recalls this period, 'I contacted some large pharmaceutical companies but they were reluctant to try anything new, they were not convinced about me or my product. They had their own in-house research
and products which took priority.' So convinced was Kartar as to the
value of his product that he remained undeterred in the face of all the
opposition. 'I was frustrated,' he recalls. 'I could not sell my invention
and I so strongly believed in it, there was nothing on the market that
worked, I knew it was a winner.' Instead, he had enough faith in
Oralcer to set up his own company in order to sell it directly. Kartar,
together with his research colleague, Dr Meyer from Hamburg, called
the new company Vitabiotics. However, it was not to be plain sailing.

Kartar then faced another hurdle. Having found the right treatment,
he lacked the financial resources to launch a business. Instead, he
worked industriously and saved his hard-earned pharmacist's wage
whilst ensuring he kept abreast of developments in his scientific
research into nutrients and vitamins. Finally in 1971, at the age of 36,
he had £8000 in savings and a working knowledge of nutrient thera-
py. He invested all his savings in a business to market his newly
patented mouth ulcer treatment both in the UK and overseas.

The banks, it appears, were not particularly helpful in the early stages
of the business. 'They were too cautious', Kartar says critically. 'I had to
rely on myself.' The UK side of the business was painfully slow but
what helped Kartar survive was that his export business had gained
momentum. The years 1972 and 1973 were tough for businesses in the
UK generally and it was a difficult time to penetrate the pharmacy

market. 'I was the first British based Indian pharmaceutical company, and it was not easy,' he recalls with dismay. The start up period was particularly difficult because, according to Kartar, 'people were not yet used to dealing with Asians as corporate heads'. This was compounded by his being a one-man band in a corporate pharmaceutical supply sector dominated by large firms.

So how did this Asian break through? 'The backbone of Asian success is that we work harder and give a greater level of service,' Kartar asserts. 'It is important to cut costs in business and Asians cut these to the core, they live modestly and are prepared to live on peanuts in order for their businesses to survive.' This shows, once again, the paradox in the Asian community. On the one hand they are ruthlessly cost conscious in their business dealings, but on the other they are the most generous and open-hearted people when it comes to charitable causes. Kartar is particularly philanthropic: 'I inherited this from my parents, they quietly gave a lot to charity, particularly women's charities.' It is also a facet of their business personality that the banks have overlooked in the past.

The Hare and the Tortoise

It was to be a slow start and initial sales of Oralcer were disappointing. Undeterred once again, Kartar took matters into his own hands, quite literally, and took to the streets, personally approaching local pharmacies. Kartar explains his methods: 'I couldn't afford sales people at the time, I had to do this by myself, plus I wanted the pleasure of selling my own product.' His cold-calling technique paid off and he eventually made his first sale in spring 1971. It was modest; despite using his pharmaceutical background and knowledge of the product to convince buyers of its worth, he only managed to sell £5-worth of Oralcer. Resilient, he continued with his personal approach of attempting to convince pharmacies to recommend Oralcer to their customers. It was a time-consuming but effective marketing strategy which not only saved advertising costs but also gave a direct and personal touch to the product. The product succeeded, slowly but surely.

Kartar's confidence grew and within a year he was ready to launch his next product, branded as Omega 11-3, a specialized multinutrient vitamin. The launch of this meant hiring his first employee, a friend in need of a job. By now his marketing had evolved from word of mouth to local press advertising. The next step was to go to the national press to raise the profile of Vitabiotics. His early methods were a struggle, and took a lot of time, but they made him realise the value of marketing. Now the Vitabiotics sign is on virtually every London bus and appears in the media regularly. It was an early and very important lesson and his strategy paid off.

Despite the slow start in the UK, Kartar found his Nigerian export business to be more successful, thus providing the ready cash required to sustain the UK business. Kartar admits that his first year was both challenging and disappointing in terms of sales figures. However, he had such faith and conviction in his products that he never contemplated giving in. Instead, he always advises caution and a softly-softly approach. The first few years after the launch of Oralcer, the company invested steadily in more vitamin and nutrient research, funded mainly from export revenue generated by sales of Omega H-3 and partly by the slow but consistent rise in the popularity of Oralcer. It was to be another six years before Vitabiotics launched its next range of products. This is a fiercely competitive industry and today vitamins are commonly available, but when Vitabiotics launched Omega H-3 it was a completely new concept. Kartar is a great believer that patience is a virtue and that the tortoise wins at the end. 'I believe in waiting for the right product to come along,' he explains. He has achieved success many times over with this approach.

Despite steady growth, stable profits and a growing organization, Kartar still found it difficult to break into the big league. His confidence was high and he was ambitious, with the energy and drive to match. In 1992, his sales team approached Boots the Chemist with an idea for two new products, Menopace and Premence, but were turned away. Once again, disappointed but undeterred, Kartar decided to focus on selling the new products through health-food stores instead. Kartar admits he was disappointed with the Boots rejection but he took it as a challenge. 'I felt I needed to do more to convince them,' he continues. 'This was the only non hormonal product, at the time, for the treatment of menopause.' Once again, he firmly believed in his product. His business acumen kicked in and he decided to focus marketing efforts by promoting the benefits of the new products through highly successful clinical trials. This is the marketing strategy the company now adopts for all its launches and it paid off handsomely, even then. The products were launched to much acclaim, and within a year Boots changed tack and decided to stock them. They were soon followed by Superdrug, Tesco and Safeway.

Where Are They Now?

Kartar is married to Rohini and has two sons and one daughter. He has delegated some of the responsibility for the company to Vitabiotics' strong management team. Keeping it in the family, this team includes his younger son Tej and his eldest son, Professor Ajit Lalvani, who has a non-executive role as Medical Director. The entrepreneur is often married to his business and Kartar is still involved in actively steering the company despite being in his seventies; he has no plans to retire. Indeed, he does not seem to be slowing down either.

Vitabiotics now exports to 85 countries worldwide with 20 brands in the UK alone, eight of which are Britain's number one in their own individual category. The company markets globally and employs 2200 people worldwide, with factories and offices in six countries. It has been successful in breaking into a difficult but lucrative US healthcare market. Kartar credits his son Tej for this breakthrough – 'we had two failed attempts at trying to enter the US market' – and it was only after Tej joined the company that they got results and managed to get their products into the US multiples. 'He dealt with the barriers effectively,'

Kartar recalls proudly. This was no mean feat as the US pharmaceutical sector does not provide easy entry for anyone, so steeped is it with bureaucracy. Vitabiotics is now focussed on building up existing brands by creating new ranges of products.

The second generation are coming up the ranks. Inspired by his father, Ajit, the elder son, has had an extraordinarily successful career as a scientist and physician. During his 15 years as a leading medical academic at Oxford University, where he also taught medicine at Magdalen College, Ajit invented the ground-breaking new blood test for the diagnosis of tuberculosis which is proving to be a crucial new weapon in the global battle against this disease. Ajit was recently awarded a Personal Chair and is a Professor in infectious diseases at Imperial College London. His achievements are close to Kartar's heart. 'Innovation and medicine have been my life and to see my son getting international recognition for his research in the fight against TB makes me proud,' he says with emotion.

Loyal to the people who got him to where he is today and with his roots firmly in his academic beginnings, in 1994 Kartar invited the internationally renowned scientist (originally his lecturer) Professor Arnold Beckett OBE to become Chairman of Vitabiotics. This served to further enhance its global reputation for its innovative capabilities under Beckett's leadership.

Making a Fortune – Kartar's Perspective

So, what are the secrets of his success? This professional, who did not start his business until he was 36 years old, has the following advice for budding entrepreneurs. Get a job in a company first within the sector you are interested in and learn as much as you can. 'Tire yourself out, be a slave to your work, see it as an opportunity to learn,' advises Kartar. 'It's the best training you will ever have.' He stresses the work ethic: 'There is no easy way, you have to work hard and love your work.'

With a mindset truly typical of many Asians, he adds, 'spend little money on yourself, and always less than your earnings. Be frugal.' The grit that has seen so many Asian entrepreneurs succeed comes through once again. 'Never be deterred if you fail or face challenges, become more determined and more involved. Look for solutions.' He recalls, 'I was never disheartened, maybe disappointed, if things didn't work out or if sales were poor.'

He has a determination to survive and not go under. This spirit has remained firm throughout his life. He is now at the top of his field but is still passionately alive and eager to continue; he can't relax. The science, the innovation and the business are in his blood: 'I suffer more than most Asians; I am more emotionally involved because I love my subject. My subject is my business.' He is probably the only notable UK Asian entrepreneur who has researched and invented his own products, patented them and then built a business on his own inventions. He was not content to work as a research scientist for a major company. This complex marriage of research science and business is an odd combination for most. 'I built my business on my own scientific innovation,' he says proudly.

Kartar has had many accolades heaped upon him including the Distinction in the Field of Science Award in 2005 from the India International Foundation UK and the DTI Science Award 2005 for innovation in HIV treatment. Kartar has ensured that all Vitabiotics products are linked with related charities and has made many contributions to the wider community.

Spreading his interests, Kartar's long-standing fascination with history has stimulated him to research and author a book featuring the lesser-known, 'other side' of the last 100 years of Britain's two centuries of colonial rule in India. This book narrates the great industrial, civil and social reforms in nineteenth- and twentieth-century India seen from the Indian point of view, and for the first time in Indian history shows people of all castes, cultures, religions and languages working together.

According to Kartar, 'In 1947, Britain left behind the world's largest sustainable democracy, with a very elaborate railway system, post and telegraph network, along with some great institutions like a unified world-class army and an excellent civil service, an impeccable judiciary, Parliament and the legacy of good governance with law and order.' This factual and illustrated account, entitled *The Making of India*, is due for publication soon. He is also fluent in several languages including English, German, Punjabi, Hindi and Sindhi, and enjoys watching cricket.

When Indian premier Indira Gandhi said, 'My grandfather once told me there were two kinds of people: those who do the work and those who take the credit. He told me to try to be in the first group; there was much less competition,' she could well have been referring to Kartar Lalvani. He has made an enormous contribution to the UK economy and yet remains steadfastly in the background. He has compassion for the human spirit which goes way beyond giving to charity or seeking honours or recognition. What Kartar gives, he gives from the heart. This encompasses his business, his family, his friends and the wider community. He has sustained his empire for many decades and continues his fortuitous rise with the new challenges ahead.

Background Reading

Yahoo India. *Gulu Lalvani's spectacular Indian-style wedding for daughter*, April 7

Sir Gulam Noon

Photo supplied by Sir G K Noon

Innovator, inspirational role model and visionary, Sir Gulam Noon has set the standard for entrepreneurship in the ethnic food market. If you have ever shopped at a major UK supermarket such as Sainsbury's, Waitrose or Morrison's, you have probably bought some of his products without even knowing it. Noon, as he is known, is the founder and guiding light of Noon Products, and has built his reputation in the food business. The company makes over 1.8 million ready meals every week and has an annual total turnover in excess of £100 million. Noon is an avid follower of cricket and a major investor in the India Room at the Oval. However, he also finds to time to internationalize the business with strong and growing export markets worldwide. Together with his other companies, Royal Sweets and Dombay Halwa, Noon has created over 1000 jobs in the UK. His personal fortune is estimated to be in the region of £70 million.

Chapter 7

Early Hardships

Born in Mumbai in 1936, Gulam Kaderboy Noon is the second eldest of three brothers and three sisters. His father was originally from Rajasthan. The debate in academic circles has been one of 'nature' or 'nurture': are entrepreneurs born or can this behaviour be taught? It has often been said that early influences are extremely important. The Noons certainly had a strong history of enterprise and have been involved with it for over a century, if that goes any way to answering the question. From as early as 1898 the Noon family were in business when Noon's grandfather opened his first Indian confectionery shop in the capital.

For a close-knit family that valued family life so much, the early years were not kind and Noon is no stranger to tragedy. He had to deal with the deaths of both his elder brother and father at a comparatively early age. His father had cardiac problems, but the death of his brother, from typhoid at the age of 26, is thought to have sent his father to an early grave. Noon was only 8 years old at the time. His mother had, by then, been widowed twice though she was only 29, and his younger sister was still a baby. The family was in emotional turmoil and had crippling medical bills. Often with adversity comes strength and Noon's mother, a woman of courage, refused to give in or sell the business. There was no alternative; young Noon had to give up his studies and join. His sacrifice meant his younger siblings could study. The sheer weight of this responsibility would have daunted a weaker person. One of Noon's first stark realizations in life was that of the importance of money.

Some people dream of success, while others wake up and work hard for it. At the age of 17, Noon inherited the confectionery business which had by now been in operation for over 100 years. Even at this early age he showed a determination to succeed and business acumen beyond his years. He thrived as a businessman and made it a success. This formed the basis of his meteoric career which was to span several decades and see Noon become one of the UK's most popular and successful Asian entrepreneurs. His family still owns the confectionery business, Royal Sweets, which has now developed into an international franchise. At first, the business was a very meagre set-up, but within ten years the annual turnover had increased tenfold. 'Life was comfortable', Noon recalls, 'but it was not enough, I was restless. I wanted bigger challenges.'

The creation of wealth is roundly applauded in the Asian culture. Temples, gurdwaras (Sikh temples) and mosques are richly decorated; the use of gold and precious gems in these places of worship is legendary. The communities are extremely generous and communal money has made many advances. This society equates wealth with success and sees it as nothing to be ashamed of. The basic driver is to succeed in life with dignity and respect, and to provide for the family. If you can help relatives and friends too, then your status is further enhanced. Wealth enables you to give.

Noon was brilliant at identifying new opportunities. He was prepared to diversify and did not limit himself, nor was he afraid of taking risks. He set up a paper conversion unit called The Paper Print and Products followed by another business, Noon Blister Packing. Noon had a thirst for knowledge, and as the businesses grew he became more and more frustrated and felt increasingly in need of a bigger platform: 'I had fire in my belly,' he recalls. He took a calculated risk in leaving Mumbai but instinct told him it was the right decision. 'I needed to learn about new technology,' he reminisces. 'There was a limit to the growth of the business in India at that time.' Mumbai is the perfect proving ground: 'If you can succeed in Mumbai then you can succeed anywhere in the world,' recalls Noon. His father and grandfather inspired him and provided the platform from which he could build. He has never forgotten this and the strength and unity of the family is integral to his business.

Noon is a man of taste and some refinement. A tall, distinguished man, in good shape for someone in his seventies, he has a positive energy and aura about him. Everything about him smacks of quality. His office is spacious, tidy and tastefully decorated. He collects fine art and there are some eye-catching eclectic pieces as you walk into his opulent office and reception areas. He is always hospitable and polite, but not a man to trifle with. Noon is passionate about cricket and has a collection of 102 signed cricket bats dating back to 1926. Much of his social life revolves around cricket; he is often spotted at matches and is a regular at the Oval.

Stepping into the UK

Noon came to the UK in the late 1960s and was mesmerised by it. He recalls, 'It was so calm and sophisticated compared to the hustle and bustle of Mumbai.' His love affair with the country, although oftentimes turbulent, has continued ever since.

He kept a foot in both countries. During this time he was exporting Indian confectionery from the Mumbai business to the UK and travelling backwards and forwards. Using his community networks, he found a British Asian partner and set up Bombay Halwa Limited, selling Indian confectionery. They opened a shop in Southall, a predominantly Asian area in west London, and soon expanded nationally. He settled permanently in England in 1971 and ran Bombay Halwa and Royal Sweets. Both continue to flourish today.

It was the Ugandan dictator, Idi Amin, who was to perversely help Noon establish the foundations for his sensational success in later life. Noon's timing was impeccable; he was in the right place at the right time. Indian sweets were a niche market in the UK but demand became strong when the East African Asian community came to England after their expulsion by Idi Amin in the 70s. Noon spotted that there might be a market for authentic Asian confectionery, and he had the expertise to produce it. His business soon expanded from two shops to twenty, all selling Indian sweets. There was still an itch he needed to scratch and, despite his success in two countries, Noon still felt that he lacked the technological knowledge needed to advance his food business. He was hungry for more.

Taking a Bite of the Big Apple

One characteristic of the Asian community is to tap into family and community networks and to exploit the 'global village'. Noon made full use of his connections and headed to the US for four years when an opportunity arose to collaborate with the Taj group of hotels, who are major players in the hotel and food business both in India and internationally. Noon was eager to take on a challenge and he hungered for knowledge and experience. Together they put up a frozen foods plant in New York opposite La Guardia airport producing Indian meals. Noon was now commuting between New York and London. Unfortunately, it was a transatlantic failure: this time he was in the wrong place at the wrong time. America did not warm to the idea, not having a history of Indian food and with only a very small Indian Asian population. Failure is a man who has blundered but is not able to cash in on the experience; Noon is not this man, and he will not use the word failure to describe this experience. He admits that he was naive and did not understand the US market and their tastes at that time. He had had bitten off more than he could chew; the venture did not work and a lot of money was lost. 'The US venture was my biggest financial disaster but was my steepest learning curve,' recalls Noon. 'There is no such word as failure if you are an entrepreneur; setbacks are lessons.' Albeit very expensive lessons, it would seem. According to author Michael Korda, 'Never walk away from failure. On the

contrary, study it carefully and imaginatively for its hidden assets.'
This Noon did.

He was undaunted, firmly believing that 'adversity brings opportunity'.
This was an invaluable learning experience: 'In the US I had undertaken a lot of research and development into the Indian food industry
and technology and learnt the art of manufacturing Indian food in
large quantities.' Equipped with this newly acquired expertise and
experience, and undeterred, he returned to England. When motivational guru Napoleon Hill wrote, 'Most great people have attained
their greatest success just one step beyond their greatest failure,' he
could have been talking about Noon. Wiser for his experience, and
equipped with his new-found technical knowledge, Noon was convinced the time was right to introduce Indian chilled and frozen foods
into the UK market. Britain, with its strong links with India and familiarity with Indian cuisine, was a safer bet. The restaurants had done
all the hard work and introduced Indian food to the British palate;
Noon wanted to take it a step further and put it on the supermarket
shelves.

So determined was he by now, still bruised by the US experience, that
he used his charisma and his excellent negotiation skills and managed
to convince Bird's Eye and then Sainsbury's and Waitrose to buy his
products. They were followed shortly by the Trusthouse Forte hotel
and restaurant chain. This was the start of a company that is now syn-
onymous with quality authentic food; Noon Products Ltd was incorporated in 1987 in England and started trading from February 1989.
The company now specializes in chilled and frozen ethnic foods such
as Indian, Chinese, Thai and Mexican.

Successful Endeavours

Noon Products is based in Southall and the company has an annual turnover in excess of £100 million per annum and makes over 1.8 million
ready meals every week in its three production facilities. The swift and

phenomenal success of Noon Products lies in Noon's ability to link with the best food retailers, the care taken with product development and technology and human resource development. The measure of his confidence is how he approached the major retailers instead of supplying small corner shops – the Bird's Eye contract alone was worth £2.7 million. Soon supermarkets were placing orders and Sainsbury's approached him to supply chilled food to their 500 outlets; this was followed by a Waitrose contract. Expansion thereafter was swift. His present customer base for his chilled and frozen food ranges include the biggest names in UK supermarkets – Sainsbury's, Waitrose, Somerfield, Aldi, Morrison's, Marks & Spencer and the independent stores Cullen's and Budgens.

It wasn't always so; supermarkets did not always stock quality food in the past. 'I started in 1988 by buying £50-worth of food from supermarkets and tasting it all,' Noon recollects. 'It was all bloody insipid, badly packaged and miles away from real Indian food. People say my firm has changed the British palate. I think they're not far wrong. But you must credit Indian restaurants too. They enabled me to put my meals on the shelf. Britain ruled India for 300 years and when we parted company it was as friends. I'd like to think I've helped amalgamate our two cultures.'

Noon attempts to retain the authenticity of the original dishes and consequently hires the finest chefs and product development managers. He concentrated on product and market development in the early stages of the business. He is always one to spot opportunities and to take advantage of trends. 'The recession is a time to expand', he asserts, 'providing you have the capital to invest in new equipment which can be purchased at favourable rates during a recession.' He built up much of his investment during the recession and growth was strong. His basic philosophy in business is to improve the quality of the product and make sure that it is packaged to as high a standard as possible. Noon Products was going from strength to strength, and Noon himself was becoming known in the community as a key entrepreneurial player. Growth brings its own challenges and the best leaders keep abreast of changes.

Management guru Peter Drucker stated, 'Management is doing things right; leadership is doing the right things'. Noon was by now at a plateau in his business career. He was satisfied with his success and had the time and space to delegate more to his executive team while he concentrated on the vision and strategic direction of the company. These are not typical Asian qualities, he observes: 'Practices that are acceptable in India cannot possibly work in the West. Asians are sometimes slow to adapt to Western business practices and so don't succeed.' He continues, 'Asians find it hard to let go and let professionals in.' Noon is different. 'I delegate well and trust people with responsibility. Some people let me down', he explains, 'which is inevitable but one cannot run a business of this size without trust and delegation.' Asian businesses per se are no different from any other business but what is important to note is that Asian businesses have some different values, ethos, culture, style and modus operandi.

Noon's level of confidence is inspiring as is the confidence he has in his team. His executive team includes both family members and outside professionals. His elder daughter, Zeenat, originally worked for the Taj Group where she was a food and beverage manager. Qualified in the food industry, she was the right person to entice into his business. 'I persuaded her to join the business,' recalls Noon. 'She is independent of me and I respect her decisions, she has her own role and identity.' Her relationship with her father is important and she finds he inspires confidence and pushes the team. 'You need someone strong to back you,' Zeenat says. When asked whether she feels she is constantly in the shadow of her father she replies, 'It is a good shadow, it protects me and enables me to grow'. This is a measure of how Noon empowers his management team and enables them to be entrepreneurial in their own right for the corporate good.

Making a Fortune – Noon's Perspective

The main reasons for the success of Noon Products are threefold: firstly, the quality of the products is higher than their competitors. The secret of success, according to Noon, is 'never sacrifice quality.' Secondly, Noon takes great pains to ensure that the plant is run using state of the art technology. No expense is spared in keeping to the highest standards of hygiene and efficiency. Thirdly, Noon has a loyal and highly trained team of managers which include his daughters Zeenat and Zarmin, and his brother Akbar Shirazi. Noon has always taken calculated risks in life. His philosophy is that if one takes ten decisions and seven of them are right then one has done really well. 'I go with my instincts. If I'm right seven our of ten times, it's enough,' he says.

His advice to others is to have a clear focus. 'Whatever you want to do, keep your eye on the ball,' he asserts. Passionate about his business, Noon counsels others to, 'fall in love with your work; be prepared to work long hours and enjoy them'. He continues, 'It's important also to have integrity in business. If you want to sustain any professional relationship long term there must be integrity and trust.' Noon is loyal to his staff and customers and has seen this returned many times. He cautions, 'Remember loyalty works two ways; Do not expect your staff to be loyal to you, if you are not loyal to them.'

Growing your venture is important. 'Keep growing, you will be adding value to the economy by generating wealth and creating jobs. If you fail to grow you are going backwards,' he asserts. 'Do not be motivated solely by money; money for money's sake is not motivation enough to overcome the many hurdles and challenges you will face. Unless you love and believe in what you do with a passion, and are prepared to work long hours there is no point setting up.' Remember, he says, 'Success has many fathers, failure is an orphan'.

Up in Flames

He was not to enjoy a smooth ride. On November 14, 1994 disaster struck when his entire factory burnt down. His 250-strong workforce were in tears and he was ruined. Noon was determined to triumph over adversity. He set about resolutely to salvage what he could. His first thoughts were for his workforce and he showed his loyalty by paying his workers for eight weeks even though they were inactive. In the chaos, with the shock and devastation of losing everything he had built up, Noon kept his cool. He was determined to build the business up again, and viewed it as a temporary setback. His pragmatic approach to damage limitation paid off and his company was soon stronger than ever. His quick thinking meant that he used all his resources. He utilized all his available assets, Bombay Halwa factories were located elsewhere and he dedicated one of these to produce orders for Noon Products. He shifted frozen food production to Wrexham in north Wales and was able to meet 80 percent of his commitments.

His single-mindedness meant that his products were back on supermarket shelves within ten weeks. Such was the loyalty and quality of customer relationships this man had inspired, that Sainsbury's and Waitrose continued their relationship with him during this turbulent period, even though other competitors saw an opportunity and approached them. Failure is clearly an attitude and not an outcome. The strength and resilience displayed by Noon during this episode was clear to see. The upshot was that he went on to build three new factories after the fire using the latest technology and the business went from strength to strength.

He made a remarkable recovery and, in August 1995, doubled his capacity and shifted his entire operations for Noon products to a brand new factory – of over 55,000 square feet – just outside London. A second plant followed, covering about 50,000 square feet, dedicated entirely to the supermarket chain Waitrose. Noon says, 'Things happen in life, it's how you react that is important.' After all, he echoes the words of Confucius, 'Our greatest test is not in never falling but rising every time we fall'.

The Phoenix Rises

Asian entrepreneurs are known for being emotionally tied to their businesses and wary of outside influences. They also face succession problems compounded by cultural restraints and traditions. Noon wanted to expand. He hungered for another factory to meet the growing vision he had for the firm but needed the capital to expand in order to realise his vision. In 1999 W T Foods made an offer to buy out Noon for £50 million and, in a shock move, Noon welcomed this offer. This went against most Asian business family norms where they strive to keep the business private. Noon realized he needed more professionalism, and did not believe in hanging onto a family concern. He had seen many second and third generations dissipate the hard work of the first generation. Furthermore, he did not want to burden his two daughters with the business. He welcomed the idea and merged with W T Foods, much to the surprise of many around him.

So in January 1999 Noon Products became part of the W T Foods Group plc, a public company quoted on the London Stock Exchange. W T Foods owned several other firms but they were all distribution companies. Needless to say, any action can result in a risk and following this merger, W T Foods suffered a sharp drop in its share price. Noon was not happy: 'There wasn't a hope in hell for the group to tap the markets for the funds required to build a major new factory.' The City did not understand the company and Noon was alarmed. The massive and sustained growth in ready meals and curries failed to register. This annoyed Noon. 'We had to do something. If we stood still, we would lose our market share,' he says. He is acutely conscious of the competitiveness of the sector. He was still looking for opportunities but felt that he would not be able to raise money from the stock market to build a new factory given the difficult economic conditions at the time.

The solution was to take the company off the market. He approached a venture capital company and a management buyout was effected in 2002 resulting in Noon buying back most of the shares from the market. Backed by private equity house Bridgepoint, W T Foods was 'released' from the City in a multimillion-pound deal. His entire conglomerate of eight companies was bought out for £126 million. Noon's role remained much as before – Chairman and Managing Director of Noon Products and Executive Director of W T Foods. 'I'm married to this business,' he says. 'All my energy is here.'

Bridgepoint immediately injected funds so he could set up his third factory which was opened by Prince Charles in 2002. This factory is wholly dedicated to Sainsbury's, Noon's largest customer. It is the only factory in the UK to have 'Micro ban' walls and floors to prevent the spread of germs. The other benefit was the number of jobs created in an otherwise deprived area.

In 2005 Noon was approached by Kerry Foods Limited to which he sold the Noon Products company, retaining the other seven companies, for £124 million. He continues to be a non-executive Chairman but professes to be unemotional about it. Noon Products is now a major international player exporting worldwide. Facilities now include the three modern state of the art factories on the same industrial park in Southall, each with a vast floor space, producing 300,000 meals per day, six days a week. They have their own laboratory accredited by Campden & Chorleywood Food Research Association for in-house testing and analysis of microbiological as well as chemical results. There is a butchery for dicing meat in accordance with customers' requirements and a separate vegetable dicing unit, both dedicated solely to Noon Products. Success is evident and turnover rose from £2.8 million in 1989 to £112 million in 2007. There are over 1000 employees working in Bombay Halwa and Noon Products combined.

Early Retirement?

A successful man never stands still and now, with more free time, Noon continues to explore other opportunities and has teamed up with business partners in property and construction. He runs a construction and property empire out of his central London management company. With a business partner, he has recently built a five-star hotel in Bahrain.

No stranger to accolades, Noon was awarded an MBE in recognition of his contribution to the food industry in 1996. His office is full of photographs of his encounters with business and political leaders including Tony Blair, Gordon Brown, Michael Heseltine, Prince Charles and the Queen. One wall in his office displays his five degree certificates. He is particularly proud of these: 'I didn't go to university but I was given these later!'

He was also the first elected non-white president of the London Chamber of Commerce in its 126-year history. In 2002 he received a knighthood in recognition of his contribution to British Industry as a whole. Noon is also an unofficial spokesman of what he calls 'the silent majority of law-abiding Muslims' in Britain. He has been a great leader for moderate Muslim thought. He was the first Muslim to make a bold statement in the *Financial Times* saying that extremist Muslims who don't like this country should leave. He feels Asians must look at politics as a career for, in the words of the philosopher Plato, 'Those hesitant to enter into politics run the risk of being governed by inferior politicians.'

He now has time to work on his Noon Foundation and his other charities. The Noon Foundation was established in December 1995, with a major donation of £4 million from his personal assets. Support is given to a wide range of UK and international causes, representing education, health, welfare and individuals in special need. These are multifaith and multicultural in origin. The Noon Foundation also sponsors university students.

Vilification without Justification

Not one to stay out of the headlines, even in his advanced years, Noon is set to face the biggest challenge of all, a stain on his character. He is embroiled in one of the biggest political scandals of recent years, the 'cash for honours' saga. It was revealed that Noon had removed a reference to his £250,000 loan to the Labour Party in official documentation for the House of Lords committee, whose job it was to approve the Prime Minister's nomination for peerages.

Noon, who so values integrity and honesty was devastated: 'I would rather fall in honour than succeed by fraud.' That is why the cash for honours scandal has hurt him so much. When asked about the peerage he said, 'I gave £250,000 as a loan and was asked not to declare it but I did declare it when I forwarded my papers to the scrutiny committee. The very next day I was asked to retrieve the form and remove the entry of £250, 000. I did this – that was a mistake. I had nothing to hide and nothing to gain by doing this.' Noon admits that the negative publicity affected his family badly. 'I am strong, I have been through a lot in life and can deal with this, but to see my family hurt was hard.' The relentless media slurs and scrutiny took their toll. 'I feel disappointment. I have done so much for the UK and I felt I have been treated very badly. I was hung, drawn and quartered before any investigation.' After a vitriolic attack lasting several months, the media have softened towards him and many now feel he was an innocent victim.

He did have some high-profile support at the time. John Selwyn Gummer MP said in his defence, 'He is a distinguished man who has been besmirched instead of honoured and I believe has been very seriously damaged entirely wrongly.' Noon himself feels that his own Asian community, with the exception of a few, was cowardly and sat back and watched. 'No one wrote letters of support on my behalf. They gloated,' he recalls. This gives an insight into the competitive, jealous side of the community. He feels he had more support from the host community who supported him publicly. He is resolute, though: 'I am confident that I have done nothing wrong so I have nothing to fear. The police interviewed me twice, I gave honest answers.' The outcome of all this is unresolved at present, but Noon holds his head up high and his conscience is clear.

For a man who has done so much to support the Labour Party in government it was a poor return. Despite his experience, he remains an avid supporter and champion of government initiatives, and has not felt held back by any bureaucracy. He is positive about public-sector initiatives and champions small- and medium-sized enterprises. He is not one to play the race card or bemoan fate. He asserts, 'All my customers, the big multiples, are British, I feel no barriers. It was an advantage being an Asian and supplying authentic Asian food.' He continues, 'Most of my workforce are Asian because of the catchment area and I have strong contacts within my own community, I will always help where I can. The UK has given me everything. It is the best country in the world to work in. Opportunities exist regardless of caste, creed and colour.'

Mahatma Ghandi once said, 'Life is not a continuum of pleasant choices, but of inevitable problems that call for strength, determination and hard work.' Noon has certainly risen to the challenge. He is a dedicated family man and is married to Mohini, who is a great supporter of any initiative Noon takes on in his charity and social work. He is very close to his two daughters Zeenat and Zarmin and dotes on his granddaughter Natania. Noon is a man at ease with himself, who has led a balanced life. He has seen ups and downs in life, is philosophical and can share his trials, tribulations and successes. Noon's future role is unclear, but what is certain is that this human dynamo has established himself as one of Britain's most honoured and respected Asian entrepreneurs.

Background Reading

Rock, S., 'What on earth is Sir Gulam Noon up to now?' *Real Business*, October 2006.

Vallely, P., 'The Saturday profile; Gulam Noon: Currying favour', *Independent* (online edition), July 15, 2006.

Vijay and Bhikhu Patel

Photo supplied by Vijay and Bhikhu Patel

Born into poverty in the western highlands of Kenya, the brothers Vijay and Bhikhu Patel arrived in the UK when Vijay was just 16 with a handful of O Levels, £5 and a determination to succeed. To pay his way through college, Vijay took any number of menial jobs before earning a place at the College of Pharmacy in Leicester. Bhikhu, meanwhile, was studying to be an architect. In 1975 Vijay opened his first pharmacy in Leigh-on-Sea, Essex. Now, together with Bhikhu, he heads one of the UK's largest pharmaceutical companies, Waymade Healthcare, which employs over 700 people. Vijay Patel is the Chief Executive and Bhikhu Patel the Managing Director of Waymade Healthcare, estimated to be worth £750 million.

Chapter 8

Early Hardship

Vijay and Bhikhu Patel were born in Kenya, where their father had settled after leaving the Gujerat area of India. Their father worked in the timber business in Kenya but sadly died when Vijay was only 6 years old and Bhikhu was just 8. Growing up impoverished in Eldoret, the Patels learned many lessons about survival and hard work. When their father died they had to make the most of Kenya, which was now the family home. India was not an option; it was full of poverty and complex relationships.

They were brought up by their mother, Shantaben, a strong character and the 'biggest inspiration in my life', according to Vijay. Life was a struggle for the family but their mother was determined that her boys would be educated. Shantaben raised her children whilst working seven days a week in a nursery. These were important days in their lives and ones that set the scene for Vijay; the Patels do not shy away from work. The three qualities Shantaben instilled in her children are, 'honesty, integrity and humility', recalls Vijay with reverence. 'She keeps me grounded, even now, "Son, you may have a few pennies in your pocket now but don't forget who you are and where you came from" are words I often hear,' he says. Her resolve paid off, Bhikhu was to become an architect and Vijay a pharmacist. More of that later.

The hardships they faced were a stark lesson for Vijay and had a profound effect on him. He knew then and there that he wanted to be rich. Unlike other children, when asked what he wanted to be, he did not say an accountant, lawyer or doctor but simply, 'I want to be rich'. He was very clear about his goal – though possibly not the route – and says, 'When you have nothing but the clothes on your back you have nothing to lose.'

The inequalities of wealth were emphasised further by the other children at school who enjoyed holidays in Mombassa, or had parents who owned cars: 'Just getting a lift in a car would get me excited. As a child you really notice what you don't have.' Showing true grit, however, Vijay did not sulk or envy others; he had a maturity beyond his years and a love and loyalty towards his mother that exceeded all else. He understood how difficult things were and instead of trying to put pressure on his mother as many children his age would have done, he tried to ease her pressure. If there was a school trip which required paying for he said 'no' without even asking her. He knew she would never deny him anything, so he did. He was man enough to understand the situation. Another example was when the kids had to bring in crayons for art at school. He knew his mother could not afford them and so just told the teacher he would not be bringing any. Poverty still haunts him: 'I don't want to be there again. I don't want my kids to go through that.' He strives to distance himself from poverty as much as possible. 'Even until a few years ago when I was a millionaire many times over, I did not feel wealthy. I carried on working hard and driving myself mercilessly.' He felt God had given him an opportunity to earn money and he took it to the maximum. Vijay had a work ethic bordering on obsession. This illustrates what many of the first generation of Asians still feel now; they cannot forget the conditions they experienced in their earlier years and just to be given the opportunity to work and earn an income is prized.

Shantaben was a strong-willed, remarkable woman. She had pride and high moral values which she instilled in her children. The principal tenets of the Asian community are based on duty, respect, honesty and loyalty. Society and families are structured around love and respect where elders are given the utmost respect and, in turn, there is no limit to what they will sacrifice for the young. Crucially, as well as the work ethic, Shantaben would not allow them to accept money, even for the chores they did for others. 'I had a lot of responsibility at an early age, but I took it in my stride,' recalls Vijay proudly. While still at school and while other children were on holiday, Vijay worked solidly throughout the holidays in a draper's shop. He was not allowed to accept money and so he did it for treats. 'I went to the cinema', he recalls with relish. 'I was so excited.'

Therein lies one of his early lessons: rewards, it seems, come in many ways. 'Although I didn't get paid for working in the draper's shop, I learnt so much,' Vijay says. It was here he first exercised the business acumen that would hold him in good stead later in life. 'It taught me discipline, a good work ethic and, crucially, gave me experience of selling and negotiating with customers.' He thrived in the business: 'I was a natural.' He had found his calling. However, the family were set to face another challenge when the country got its independence from the British. In Kenya, people who did not have Kenyan citizenship had to leave. The majority of Asians had UK passports and so the choice was either to go back to India or venture into the UK. 'We saw no prospects in India as we had escaped from dire poverty there and so the only option was the UK. I felt it had more opportunity for growth,' recalls Vijay. It was a turbulent time when Vijay and Bhikhu left Kenya in 1967. Though still in their teens – Vijay was 16 and Bhikhu 18 years old – they promised their mother they would send for her after they had made their fortunes.

'I arrived in the UK on a 707 BOAC jet and my first impressions were lots and lots of Lego-like houses, all identical and so small,' remembers Vijay. He had never flown before and thought, 'What have I come to here?' Like the other Asian immigrants at that time, he had little choice. 'I did not look back, and I got on with it. I was here for a purpose – a better future for me and my family. I worked my arse off and went forward. After all, I knew I couldn't get any lower than where I had been.' It is this strength of character and resolve that has sustained him all these years.

The Land of Opportunity

The brothers were not afraid of the future. 'When you start from zero, there is nothing to compare,' says Vijay, 'You have only one way to go and that's up. There was a hunger in my belly to succeed. My brother and I were determined to better ourselves and Britain was the land of opportunity.' They were full of confidence and optimism, and were eager to make their mark.

So the teenage Vijay, armed with a few O levels, set out to study during the day and worked at night. There was really no risk. 'I arrived with the shirt on my back; that was all I could lose,' he says, philosophically. However, he had ingrained in him a deeper set of values: 'My priority was to study. I had to have a professional qualification, I had to make my mum proud.' He was conscious of how much she had sacrificed for him and says, 'I had to do this. I was single-minded.' Education, as a key to the future, is greatly valued in the Asian community and a lot of emphasis is placed on professional qualifications. Many sacrifices are made in the pursuit of academic excellence and even to this day Asian children are under a lot of pressure to do well academically.

Despite his pursuit of academic glory to please his mother, Vijay concedes that he is a trader, businessman and entrepreneur. He never wanted to work for someone else, so although he was studying to become a professional his real desire was to be rich and the only way to achieve that was through business. 'This is why I did not go into medicine or dentistry. I chose pharmacy. I could visualise myself with a shop, selling, making money. I can't, with my hand on my heart, say that I set out to cure cancer or to develop drugs that would save lives, I went into it from a business angle – the rest is incidental,' he explains.

Vijay enrolled at a London college and studied physics, chemistry and biology whilst washing dishes in a restaurant at night to earn money. He gained a degree at the College of Pharmacy in Leicester in the

Midlands. 'My mother still wanted me to be a doctor but there was no money in it. Only as much as one person can earn with their time. I wanted a first-class profession and to be a businessman. It was in the blood. I was psyched up to succeed. I did not want to save the world or win a Nobel Prize; I wanted to focus on business,' he admits. He dreamt of running his own pharmacy.

He met his wife, Smita, while studying and she has supported him unfailingly ever since and understood his relentless ambition. Smita and Vijay married soon after he left college. In the early days he told her, 'I love you, but don't stand in the way of my business' – she didn't, and is a dedicated supporter. They have two sons, a doctor and a chartered accountant. 'I want them to have the same fire in their belly and hunger that I had, albeit they have enjoyed a more privileged upbringing, ' Vijay says. He is, of course, ridiculously proud of them, 'but they don't hunger to take my business to the next level'. The son who is a doctor currently works in the pharmaceuticals industry trying to gain some wider skills and knowledge, so he may be the next Waymade apprentice.

Financial Pressure

Both Vijay and Smita worked and saved after their studies, but could not afford to buy the pharmacy Vijay so craved: 'I wanted to borrow £6000 to buy a business but the banks turned me down.' He had no collateral, no experience, no money. 'They could not see the fire in my belly and my desire to succeed, banks did not want to know me at the beginning but they are your best friends once you're established, they can't do enough,' he says, and continues, 'Banks look for two things, collateral and experience. You need to demonstrate that you are paying back loans. Once they see you are a sound business, they love you. You have a history.' Things are different now, according to Vijay: 'It's easier now to start up as banks have dedicated advisors. I never approached any other institutions, in particular public bodies, I did not need to. I did it on my own merit.' The banking world has woken up to the business merits of the Asian community and many initiatives are in place to offer good service to this entrepreneurial minority that has so made its mark on the UK economy.

After being initially rejected by several banks, Vijay was stuck but not despondent. He turned to his family networks: 'I spoke to an uncle who guaranteed the loan but for 15 percent of the business.' With this money, Vijay bought a pharmacy in Leigh-on-Sea, Essex, which he has kept to this day both for sentimental reasons and for a more practical one – it enables him to keep in touch with customer needs. He and his wife remain hands-on and are often seen working there, even today. Within his first year, he had doubled the business, and this trajectory continued. 'I had that much determination and resolve and fire. Within six months I had paid back my uncle handsomely,' he says with pride .

With growing confidence Vijay purchased another pharmacy and then another. Within five years, he had five pharmacies. The banks had now changed their view of him. 'In the 1970s it was difficult as banks did not recognise entrepreneurship,' recalls Vijay. 'They did not recognise Asians with ambition and they did not understand how much of our own time, money and emotion we put in. We would never have let the venture fail.' This passion is hard to quantify and does not fit into any credit-rating formula. The banks were conservative: 'they wanted me to consolidate the businesses and reduce risk'. Vijay felt they viewed him as some kind of wide boy. Despite not getting formal support from the government or banks Vijay had a high degree of self-belief. 'I totally believed in my ideas. After all I only had my shirt to lose,' he grins.

Like his mother before him, he worked seven days a week and became a part of the community. He had taken over the first pharmacy from an elderly English gentleman who was known and loved by everyone. It was a tough act to follow and Vijay ensured that he greeted each customer by name and tried to get to know them. His entrepreneurial spirit continued to flourish. He was always looking out for opportunities. During the 1977 Silver Jubilee celebrations, Vijay thought, 'How can I make money out of this?' He then volunteered to take photographs of the street parties. This gesture was not without motive, as all his pharmacies developed photographs. He was easily able to develop and sell the celebration photographs as souvenirs. 'I encouraged people to enlarge them and so could charge higher prices,' he admits sheepishly. He spotted opportunities everywhere. From 1970 to 1980 Vijay prospered and now had a chain of pharmacies. 'Growth was strong but what I lacked in the organization was financial discipline,' he acknowledges.

Bhikhu Joins the Business

Cue his brother, Bhikhu. Bhikhu had studied to be an architect and was doing well. He had a fine mind, was shrewd, arty and, like Vijay, had ambition, but he was not making big money as an architect. 'I got him into the business,' says Vijay. 'I needed financial discipline and I needed someone I could trust.' Bhikhu fitted the bill: 'He was my blood and my brother, trust was utmost.' For many Asians, the first loyalty is to their family. Bhikhu recalls his decision to enter the business. 'It was not difficult. For a time, I was a civil servant but things did not happen quickly enough, so I took the opportunity to join my brother. As for architecture, I'm still building. Only now it's a growing business rather than libraries or shopping malls.'

On Bhikhu joining the business, they made a pact – Vijay would make the money and Bhikhu would look after it. To this day the formula is sound. It is the ideal partnership. Bhikhu puts sanity into the business; he keeps it grounded and, according to Vijay, 'he makes my ideas and innovations real'. He acts as a reality check. Bhikhu supports Vijay but gives honest feedback and – crucially – 'as my older brother I respect him'. Both brothers are married with children and live near each other in Essex. Their mother lives with Vijay. 'My brother and I have built up this business together. I simply couldn't have done it without him,' claims Vijay. This illustrates the strength and unity of the family which is the backbone to many Asian business success stories.

Vijay is tall, well dressed and has a youthful energy about him, a good-looking man who smiles easily and is charming but astute, kind but sharp. He is a man who is comfortable with his success but still finds it novel enough and enjoys the limelight it brings. Bhikhu is two years older, the quieter and more conservative one of the two. However, don't be fooled by the demeanour of the accountant, for beneath lies a man who is just as ambitious and who focuses his sharp brain to strive confidently forward.

It was a crucial time for Bhikhu to enter, the infancy stage of the business, right at the start of the growth phase. 'This is when real expertise is required. Vijay is good on the entrepreneurial and sales side, but I am stronger on the financial and administrative side. After all, the devil is in the detail. I put discipline into the business,' Bhikhu explains. He is different from your typical City financial accountant whose job it is to balance the books. Instead he sees himself as more of an entrepreneurial accountant, involved with decisions regarding the value and growth of the business. 'I use an entrepreneurial financial approach to the business,' he explains. Bhikhu has a vision of the future and is always trying to add value and grow the business. He tries to assess the most efficient utilization of cash and resources: 'I look at where the growth should be. I am prepared to pay over the market price if need be, just to acquire the right resources. No City accountant would do that.'

Bhikhu has a sharp entrepreneurial mind of his own and he tries to spot opportunities. He has the energy and drive to stay ahead of trends: 'I try to anticipate the changes in legislation in the market.' The Patel brothers were among the first to spot the legislative changes in Europe and how this could aid the growth of their business. Noticing this opportunity led to enormous growth and was a turning point for the company. 'Our vision widened. Initially the company was set up for trading, now it has gone global', adds Vijay. Bhikhu's talents for spotting opportunities continued to be as sharp as ever: 'I spotted the opportunities during the Thatcher era. Mrs T. was good at reducing prices for pharmaceuticals.' It was another golden opportunity.

The Bureaucratic Hurdle

One of the main headaches in the business is the overwhelming bureaucracy they have to deal with. 'Legislation is a huge problem, especially in the European context. We have to take care we do not fall foul of any laws,' explains Bhikhu. This means complying with trade barriers, health and safety regulations amongst others. The system is overly bureaucratic, according to Bhikhu. 'Human rights legislation is worthy in that it is there to protect rights and stop abuse and this is particularly the case where drugs are concerned. However, sometimes it's too pedantic and really is a case of bureaucracy gone mad.'

Complying with these rules and regulations is a constant and costly challenge to the business: 'We need to employ people to fill out the never-ending paperwork and work with our legal team.' Bhikhu feels strongly there needs to be fewer barriers and less bureaucracy. One example of this excess is that every pharmaceutical product must have labels in Braille suitable for the visually impaired. There are millions of pharmaceutical products on the market and all must comply with this regulation. 'These types of blanket rules are preposterous', says Bhikhu, 'given the small proportion of the community they benefit, you have a situation where the value is small compared to the enormous costs and hassle.'

He continues, 'We seem to be legislation mad in the UK.' He does concede that whilst the UK and Europe are less stringent than the US, they could still be better: 'We need more freedom to operate, there are too many rules and regulations and too many types of taxation. We need simplification.' It is a challenge for businesses to get through these barriers. They are the same across the board for all businesses, not just Asian-owned ones. However, given the abhorrence of Asians to anything bureaucratic, perhaps they present a greater challenge to them and can be more frustrating.

So Bhikhu Patel, the entrepreneurial financial wizard, is the restraining arm in the outfit. His entrepreneurial skills complement those of Vijay and although he may be the cautious one he does not lack ambition, 'I am more realistic in what we can achieve. I am the more cautious of the two but we get more successes and more hits because of this,' he says pragmatically.

Bigger and Bigger

Business boomed and spurred the growth of a chain of outlets, and then the supply of a range of prescription medicines to retail pharmacies across the UK, heralding the birth of Waymade Healthcare in 1984. The distribution side of the business grew consistently throughout the 80s and 90s with an increasingly wide range of products offered to more and more customers. The company now supplies pharmaceutical products to wholesale and retail pharmacies, including all of the well-known high-street names, as well as to hospitals and even directly to GP surgeries. Vijay is extremely proud of the high levels of service Waymade provides to all its customers, and is grateful to the many loyal and long-serving employees who have contributed to the company's successes. With sales now exceeding £250 million per annum, Waymade has an impressive record of growth and it continues to evolve. Since the mid-90s it has built a portfolio of its own products both in the UK and, more recently, internationally.

The birth of this enterprise, Waymade Healthcare plc, came from a practical, sensible idea. It is currently one of the UK's largest pharmaceutical groups: 'I had no idea when I started it how much it would grow,' says Vijay. Waymade Healthcare was set up in order to meet the needs of the growing pharmacy chain in the way of supply, and to increase efficiency. 'It was set up primarily to meet the needs of my own pharmacies and to supply other independents,' explains Vijay. He found he was in a good position to negotiate deals. He could bulk-buy at a good discount and so everyone benefited. Having a company meant he could do this more formally. They expanded into buying and supplying medicines for their own chain as well as to hospitals and wholesalers.

The company has developed through the value chain. It has gone from retail to wholesale to sales and marketing and to development. They buy their own products and drugs and also develop their own drugs. If you look at the value chain, development and research are vital to the business. Waymade Healthcare plc consists of three main arms. Waymade, which deals with the importation and distribution of branded pharmaceuticals from Europe; Sovereign Medical, which markets a range of their own-brand and third-party generic products to the distribution chain and Amdipharm, which markets their own-brands and patent-protected products to primary and secondary care prescribers.

Vijay and Bhikhu continue to develop the company through overseas expansion and development of the wholesaling and distribution business; the target is to create a mini-Glaxo. In meeting the goal the brothers have created Amdipharm, a pharmaceutical company which aims to develop and launch new drugs as well as taking over and marketing established products. This company will target smaller segments such as palliative or critical care. Amdipharm opens a new chapter in a remarkable entrepreneurial success story. It has grown rapidly through the acquisition of products and already has a presence in 50 countries and has acquired products from a number of well-known multinational pharmaceutical companies. It is now significantly expanding its portfolio of products and has funding in place to support an exponential growth in its acquisition programme as Vijay works towards his vision of building a worldwide pharmaceutical company. Ask him if he is satisfied with the tremendous achievements of his company to date and he will tell you 'we ain't even started yet!'

Vijay and Bhikhu spotted an opportunity to acquire, develop and market new chemical entities and formulations that major pharmaceutical companies release as they consolidate and focus on large disease areas. This consolidation might arise from a number of factors including market dynamics, merger and acquisition or through competition legislation. 'Amdipharm specialises in developing medicines that meet real clinical needs but which have small-to-medium sized markets and therefore aren't a priority for major drug companies,' explains Vijay.

Amdipharm will be one of the few privately owned pharmaceutical companies and is totally self-funded – a reflection of its parent company's success as well as the fact that much of the costly support infrastructure is already in place. 'We do not currently require further financial investment,' adds Bhikhu, 'rather, Amdipharm is actively seeking product and corporate acquisitions as well as licensing opportunities to expand its portfolio.'

The brothers soon moved 'backwards' along the supply chain and began importing pharmaceuticals. They have since added a high-margin line of own-brand drugs and a relatively new pharmaceutical development arm. Eventually, they want to create a fully-fledged pharmaceutical company. The move away from distribution towards the own-brand range has seen profits increase.

Making a Fortune – Vijay and Bhikhu's Perspective

So what is the secret of the Patel brothers' success? Vijay confesses, 'I would be a nightmare employee. I always question everything, I am naturally innovative. I constantly ask, Why not? Why can't things be done differently, better? I try and invent, I generate ideas, and I love challenges.' He is very easily bored: 'I realised I would not fit into a corporation.' So is it his rebellious nature that's the successful ingredient behind his phenomenal entrepreneurial success?

His formula is simple: set up the concept or have the idea, have your team check its feasibility and assess the risks from every angle – and then make your move. 'I'm like a dog with a bone until I put the idea to bed,' he admits. 'The team know when I'm onto something, I want it delivered on time as discussed and arranged.' He is nurturing and supportive of his staff: 'I am happy if people fulfil their commitments and I can trust them to put in the effort. I don't mind delays and mistakes as long as the effort is sincere. I hate malingerers.' Vijay encourages innovation and improvement, too: 'I encourage mistakes, employees are not penalized for honest mistakes or errors, as they learn and grow. I do not want to stifle them. I support them even if they are wrong. If they are right six out of ten times then it's OK. I want empowered employees around me.' He firmly believes that you throttle the entrepreneurial spirit if you are too stern.

Bhikhu adds, 'If you have an idea for a business, no matter what it is, do not be shy of going forward, believe in yourself.' He cautions, 'Having said that, it is important to do your research well and know the business and the sector intimately. Most businesses fail due to lack of adequate research or the entrepreneurs don't know how the market will react or how consumers will react. Do your homework carefully.' Bhikhu continues, 'It is important to get expertise and advice early on, particularly in marketing. You do need to conduct detailed market research, don't automatically assume there is a market for your product. It's important not to penny-pinch with respect to good advice and advisors. It will save you a fortune in the long run.' He speaks from experience. 'The other piece of valuable advice is to set yourselves realistic goals. Overambitious ideas rarely work.'

The advice they both give budding entrepreneurs is to 'never, ever give up'. They stress that even if you encounter several calamities, it is important to keep going forward and to face your hurdles head on. It is rewarding both financially and emotionally. In addition, 'It's important to give a lot of thought to the business before starting up whether it's a market stall, product or service.' After all, 'You must know your business.' Another crucial element is understanding and defining your customer: 'You need to establish who they are. You must know more about your customers and their needs than they do.' The core Asian belief of hard work is invaluable. 'The harder you work for free launching the business, the more work you put into it the more rewarding it is.' The brothers also stress that you need to do your homework on location, the competition and the market. Only then should you make an informed decision. Bhikhu adds, 'It's also vital to get other people involved who have the skills and expertise you lack. In business, entrepreneurs have to realise that they are not good at everything. They are only interested in "non-detail" stuff. Therefore, they need better people around them dedicated to the different areas and skills they don't have. For example, you may need a good accountant or a dedicated sales person. You need experts around you as each functional area requires 100 percent attention. If one person tries to do everything, he can't, he may only put 30 percent effort, not 100 percent, into each task.' Having others in place frees entrepreneurs to continue pursuing their vision.

So why do people fail in business? 'Many people fail as they lack the skills and they don't have appropriate partners,' explains Bhikhu. This problem is compounded in the Asian community as they don't always want to pay for advice. Once you have the right partner with the right ability and knowledge and they share your vision then you are on the right road. He continues, 'It's also important to know that you may need different skills and thus people at different stages of your business. Recognize this.'

There is no shortage of entrepreneurs in this country, but few get to the next stage. Despite the success stories of wealth and achievement, many Asians never made it beyond one shop. 'They want to keep everything in-house and that is not conducive to growth,' says Vijay. 'The Asian mindset makes it doubly hard to grow a business and let go due to issues of lack of trust, suspicion and jealousy. They have a survival mentality which is good and bad, they will always save first.' The Asian community tends to be less trusting, it appears, and they resist employing personnel from outside the family – a particular problem with the first generation. This mindset hinders growth, and is not conducive to building bonds and retaining loyal staff.

Vijay is a hands-on manager with his 700 employees, 'My vision should perpetuate throughout the whole company, at every level. I walk the shop floor each day. I know what football teams my workers support, I know them.' His advice on managing staff is simple: 'give them good working conditions and pay them a fair wage'. He is convinced this promotes job satisfaction, lowers staff turnover, improves loyalty and attracts good-quality newcomers and says, 'employees who feel highly valued are more productive and nurturing talent is important for a growing business'. Staff must feel empowered and they must be given responsibility and trusted to get on with the job as only then can a business grow. 'I want to satisfy them financially because once they work for me, I demand 24 hours a day. I want a return,' says Vijay. Interestingly, he adds, 'I have noticed that if there is any overtime, Asian women are the first to volunteer. They will never say no if offered the opportunity to earn more money. Work has a greater value than leisure.'

Giving Back to the Community

The brothers are easily recognizable now from their various appearances on TV, at awards ceremonies and even have their portraits in the National Portrait Gallery. 'I am neurotic about success,' admits Vijay. 'Wealth gives you the freedom to do philanthropic works.' This gets to the core value system of the Asian mindset. He says, 'I don't gamble, I don't waste.' Asians, no matter how wealthy, generally abhor waste.

They have not forgotten their roots. Kenya is where they were born and spent their formative years under the guidance of their mother, Shantaben. They have donated a school to the local community in Eldoret. They also have their spiritual roots in the Gujerat area of India and make frequent visits there. The Waymade fortune funds schools in Kenya and regular medical camps in India.

Although money is important, Vijay in particular thrives on the recognition and accolades. The reception area of Waymade boasts a gallery of awards and these keep coming. The Patels are an outstanding example of UK entrepreneurship at its very best. They put their success down to a hunger forged in part by the sacrifices of their childhood. Their key business messages focus on driving down costs and knowing customers' requirements intimately. At the same time their management style allows them to see their workmates as colleagues, many of whom are also their friends. They have built a world-class business with consistent financial growth from humble beginnings that competes with the largest global players.

Lord Swraj Paul

Photo supplied by Lord Paul

Steel magnate Lord Swraj Paul, Chairman of Caparo Group, is a leading light and patriarch of UK Asian businesses. He is an active member of the House of Lords, firmly committed to promoting social and education policies. Born in Jalandhar, India in 1931, he married Aruna Vij in 1956 and they have three sons, one daughter, and another daughter who is sadly deceased. Lord Paul was educated at Punjab University. He then studied at the Massachusetts Institute of Technology (MIT), in the US from which he graduated with a Masters degree in Mechanical Engineering. He left MIT in 1952 to join the family business in India, Apeejay Surrendra Group, which was founded by his father. He came to the UK in 1966 to seek medical aid for his younger daughter Ambika who was seriously ill; following her tragic death he decided to stay and work in the country and founded Caparo. Caparo is best known for its ability to acquire and turn around existing businesses. Today the Group's interests include steel, engineering, materials testing and hotels. Paul's three sons, Ambar, Akash and Angad, are responsible for the day-to-day running of the group but Lord Paul chairs the board of the company he founded, with Angad at the helm as Chief Executive. The company has seen phenomenal growth and is valued at an estimated $1.5 billion.

Chapter 9

Humble Beginnings

In the year that Mahatma Gandhi made his epic salt march to defy British rule in India, 1931, 'Swraj', meaning 'freedom', was born in Jalandhar in the state of Punjab into a family of seven siblings. His mother died in childbirth when he was just 7 years old and his father, Payare Lal, died when he was 14. Raised by his eldest brother, Stya, the young Paul remained optimistic despite these tragedies. 'I have happy childhood memories,' he recalls. Payare Lal's early influence has shaped Swraj Paul's life and values. He recalls that his father 'was a fine man, very principled and a great disciplinarian who insisted that the family took all their meals together'. He instilled respect for even the most menial work, making his children clean the factory floor. 'He did not want us to consider anything beneath our dignity.' From his father, Lord Paul and his brothers learnt three important business lessons: the importance of integrity, hard work and the value of close family ties.

In 1910 his father had started out by making steel buckets, tubs, trunks and agricultural implements in a small foundry at the back of the family home. These were the humble beginnings of the Apeejay Surrendra Group which today covers a wide range of industries.

Though the business prospered, the family continued to live frugally, following the Hindu prescription 'simple living and high thinking'. When Lord Paul's mother was asked why she wore no jewels, she would proudly declare 'my sons are my jewels'. This ethic of close family ties continued and Lord Paul attributes much of his business success to the moral and emotional support he received from his three brothers – Stya, Jit and Surrendra, and the happy home life created by his wife, Aruna.

It was this resilience in the face of pain and a tenacity for accomplishment that took Paul beyond Jalandhar. He was set for even greater achievements. 'I learned to speak English at the age of 10', he says, proudly. After attending local schools he went to Foreman Christian College in Lahore to study sciences but this was a time of great turmoil for the country. It was at the time of partition, so Paul was forced to complete his studies in Jalandhar once Lahore was officially in Pakistan. He continued his studies at the Massachusetts Institute of Technology (MIT) in Boston. He left MIT with Bachelor's and Master's degrees in engineering and was later awarded the prestigious Corporate Leaders Award, the MIT equivalent of an honorary Doctor of Philosophy.

Building a Dynasty

With family pressure mounting for him to find a bride, Paul married the woman of his choice. He returned to the family business, Apeejay, in India but, he grins, 'I did not succumb to an arranged marriage despite family pressure'. Instead he married Aruna after a whirlwind romance and has been with her ever since. The marriage was not without drama ,as one would expect with Paul; he swept Aruna off her feet during a party she attended with her then fiancé! Their marriage has not only endured but has given him the stability and strength to found his dynasty. Both staunch believers in family unity and strength, their enduring partnership is an accolade to them. They have twin sons, Ambar and Akash, a daughter, Anjli, and their youngest son is Angad. The boys were educated at Harrow and Anjli went to Roedean. Paul is a devout Hindu and follows the Hindu faith. 'I pray every morning and do not eat meat or drink alcohol,' he insists. Like his father, Paul has been a stern disciplinarian to his children.

Having lost his parents at a young age, Paul's second daughter, Ambika, tragically died in 1968. The struggle to find her effective medical treatment brought Paul, Aruna and their children to England in 1966 when Ambika needed medical treatment for leukaemia. Sadly she died two years later and Paul decided to stay in England to be close to her memory despite the flourishing family business in India. The impact of her death was so devastating that it has shaped much of his life. The tragedy hit hard and Paul thought he would never recover: 'I stayed in London, not for professional reasons but because I decided to take *sanyas* [prayers] and went into meditation for about two years. I was not of this world.' He finally made peace with himself and regained the strength to carry on. 'It was Ambika who started it all,' recalls Paul sadly. 'She was an angel who changed my life.' This was a poignant and traumatic event in the life of Swraj and Aruna. Her legacy is such that she is a part of everything the Pauls do.

He threw himself into his work. His strength of character enabled him to cope with the grief and he recovered his drive and determination to succeed. The birth of their son Angad in 1970 brought a lot of joy to the family. So the Pauls remained in England after Ambika's tragic death and everything he has since created in the Caparo Group is a dedication to her memory. In 1994 Lord Paul took the opportunity to commemorate the rebuilding of London's Children's Zoo in her name.

The Development of an Empire – Caparo Industries

In 1968 Paul started his business in a one-room office in Chiswell Street in the City of London. He arranged a loan of £5000 from Glyn Mills Bank (now part of the Royal Bank of Scotland) and started to trade in steel, 'a business I was familiar with in India'. With that Hindu prescription of 'simple living, high thinking' manifested in his work, he reinvested all his profits in the business and lived modestly. His

next step was to open up his own small three-man factory called
Natural Gas Tubes in Huntingdon, making steel pipes. These were the
modest beginnings of Caparo in the late 1960s, and they provided the
basis for consolidation in the 70s. His next moves were important;
there was a recession in the UK and nobody was investing in industry.
Paul started to buy ailing companies, modernizing them and turning
them into profitable ventures.

After the 1973 oil crisis Paul decided to set up a business challenging
British Steel's steel pipes monopoly. It was like a mosquito fighting an
elephant. His vision and confidence made his company a competitor
to British steel despite its tiny size. 'I was fortunate in meeting the
Labour MP Michael Foot at this time,' Paul recalls. 'I was thinking of
building a plant in his constituency in Wales.' He remembers Michael
Foot saying to him that it the treated them properly, the Welsh people
were really wonderful. He was right. The result was a factory in Wales
with grants from the European Community. Michael Foot so inspired
Paul that he joined the Labour Party in 1974 and has been a staunch
supporter ever since.

Paul managed to raise the £5 million needed to build the new plant in
Tredegar, Wales which was opened by Prince Charles in 1977. He was
honoured by a visit from Indian Prime Minister and close friend,
Indira Gandhi, who opened an extension to the factory in 1978. This
was done against a back-drop of great economic difficulty; Margaret
Thatcher became the new Prime Minister and oil prices were at a high –
$40 a barrel. In addition, banks were not financing the manufacturing
industry, and there were problems with workers; the trade unions
were powerful.

Acquisition and Growth

While the 70s were essentially spent consolidating the business, opening new factories and mills and forming Caparo Group as the holding
company for all his activities, the 80s were more of an acquisitive

phase. The group has grown, aided by takeovers which have been both daring and hostile. Many would say that what at the time may have seemed like a small business venture actually regenerated the engineering industry in the UK. Paul is proud of this. He has often been described as 'the man who made British manufacturing industry fashionable'. It was this innate sense of opportunism, and an ability to gauge precisely when to make a business move, that led Caparo Group to begin its acquisition phase in the 80s – a period when the company was to grow beyond the confines of Britain's economy, expanding into both India and the US.

Business Hiccups

It wasn't always smooth running, though. Caparo Industries took over the consumer electronics group Fidelity in 1984 for £14 million. This business acquisition turned out to be a disaster; when Caparo took the helm they found that the published accounts were badly wrong. Investigations revealed glaring inaccuracies in stock, and asset valuations that were much overstated. So Caparo took Fidelity's accountants Touche Ross (now Deloitte & Touche) to court claiming that the company's audited accounts were not in accordance with the true state of the company. The case went to the House of Lords but Caparo lost because the ruling concluded that an auditor's responsibility was to the company and not its shareholders. Subsequently Fidelity itself initiated legal proceedings against the auditors for negligence and this time Touche Ross settled out of court.

Watch Out, the Mighty Titan is Coming!

India is the largest growth market for Caparo today, but Paul's early involvement with India was not without drama. Swraj Paul is better known in India for having threatened the monopoly of the Indian big business houses. He was persuaded to invest in India by an acquaintance and initially decided to invest 10 million rupees in two Indian blue-chip companies – DCM and Escorts. DCM's diverse range of products included food, clothing and mini-computers whereas Escorts produced tractors, motorcycles and shock absorbers. It was only when Paul learnt how vulnerable the two companies were that his predatory instincts took over and he decided to raise the sum invested to 130 million rupees (about £1.5 million). Paul tried to imitate the formula he had used to such good effect in the engineering industry in Britain whereby he identifies under-valued and mismanaged companies, buys a strategic stake and then launches a full-scale bid. He had acquired several British engineering companies in this way and both DCM and Escorts fitted the pattern.

However, Paul had not bargained on the Indian business houses' response. The business community were alarmed and joined ranks against him in fear of being the next targets for takeover by this non-resident Indian. The managements of DCM and Escorts refused to register his shares as they feared a takeover. This sparked an international scandal over the rights of non-resident Indians. The nation was divided, with the big industrialists on one side wanting to maintain their protected monopoly status and the small, entrepreneurial businesses and consumers on the other, desperately wanting a more open, liberal economy.

Paul's alliance with the late premier Indira Gandhi had always been under close scrutiny. She had, at one time, offered him a ministership in India or, if he wanted to stay in England, to make him the Indian High Commissioner in London, but he declined her offers. Instead he helped her throughout her political career and was careful not to involve her in his corporate battles. However, tragedy was to rear its ugly head once more and Paul was devastated when Indira Gandhi was assassinated during this period. She was shot by two of her Sikh bodyguards on October 31, 1984 in retaliation for the storming of the Sikh Golden Temple in Amritsar, the holiest of Sikh shrines. India was in disarray. Her son, Rajiv, supported the Indian business houses. Paul was furious and accused them of being 'cosy, self-perpetuating clubs dedicated to cheating shareholders'. He later sold his shareholdings at a loss.

The impact of Paul's challenge was to resonate throughout the Indian economy for years to come. For the first time the monopoly had been exposed, shying away from the possibility of economic growth in a vain attempt to pander to the privileged few. Over time India began to open up its economy to the world, benefiting both itself and other nations. Caparo was in the forefront of this liberalization, expanding its operations to Gurgaon with the Caparo-Maruti project, a manufacturer of pressings.

Through Paul's courage to challenge India's status quo in the early part of the 1980s, the Caparo Empire was beginning to take shape. India's economy is arguably much indebted to Paul's lead on truthfulness and fidelity in business during this period and the country recognised her debt by awarding him the Padma Bushan, the highest of honours the country can bestow on a person, and the first time that this had been awarded to a foreign citizen.

Currently 60 percent of Caparo's business is in the UK, 35 percent in the US and about 5 percent in India. Caparo is concentrating on the growing Indian market and is sure to see an increasing contribution there within the next five years. Caparo's development in India began in 1994 with Caparo Maruti, a joint venture with India's largest car manufacturer, Maruti Udyog. Caparo Maruti manufactures automotive body panels at its facility in Gurgaon (Haryana). The success of this plant has been followed by a further stamping facility at Halol (Gujarat) and Bawal (Haryana).

In the last three years Caparo has built 15 plants and there are 16 more under construction. Making further forays into India, it has bought 100 acres of land in Haryana for development of six new engineering ventures for its vehicle products' India division. The company already operates two stamping plants in the region through a joint venture with Maruti Suzuki. The new ventures will support the growth of automotive original equipment manufacture in the region including Honda cars, Honda scooters and motorcycles. Caparo has also acquired 125 acres at Sriperumbudur near Chennai. In India, Caparo's activities are focused on the automotive components sector and products include pressings, fasteners, aluminium castings, forgings, tubing and tubular components.

The Caparo School of Manufacturing Excellence in Jalandhar is a project supported by the Ambika Paul Foundation, a charitable trust set up in memory of Paul's daughter. The school, which opened its doors to students in August 2007, is in collaboration with selected UK-based universities to provide engineering, manufacturing and management education. It is the only university in the region that will conduct engineering courses in these disciplines. The courses will equip young engineers will the skills required to become absorbed in industry, both in India and abroad.

Into the US

Paul was eager to spread his wings and fortunately his ventures into the United States were to prove more profitable. His other defeats had spurred him on to newer and greater ventures. The Bull Moose Tube Company turns steel coils into tubes and pipes for products like exercise machines, lawnmowers and patio furniture. It was a division of National Intergroup and was profitable but not expanding. In 1988 National Intergroup put its tubing division up for sale. This provided the perfect opportunity for Paul, who was looking for a way to expand his interests in the US. This deal was small for National Intergroup but provided a major inroad to the US for Paul. Paul had now found his way into the US manufacturing industry and, by 1989, had acquired structural tube manufacturers Bock Industry, a company that nicely complemented Paul's company Natural Gas Tubes.

With these acquisitions in hand, Paul was once again ready to revolutionize an industry that had previously been in decline. Since he took over Bull Moose, growth and expansion have been phenomenal. His expertise in turning companies around through cost cutting and greater efficiency measures have paid off handsomely. He has created opportunities missed by other metal bashers.

Acquiring these new products meant that Paul could push Bull Moose to export more of its products. At the same time Paul innovatively expanded incentive-based pay throughout the company. Top managers receive phantom stock that pays dividends, but can only be sold to the company at a formula price. Hourly workers got incentive pay, calculated daily, based on specific performance benchmarks for each product. The unions agreed to accept the incentives. The result was that productivity increased – and so did workers' incomes.

The Man Himself

Swraj Paul has managed to harness the best qualities associated with the West, such as discipline and the honouring of commitments, with those of the East, such as magnanimity and family values. He has not shied away from takeover bids both in India and Britain, often encountering fierce opposition. He is a tough negotiator and skilled corporate fighter. He is not extravagant and lives on his salary as chairman of Caparo Group. He asserts that he is prouder of Caparo as a manufacturing group than he is of his wealth. By taking over failing industries, turning them around and then acquiring other related industries he built up the Group into the conglomerate that it is today.

In 40 years Caparo has grown from one small factory in Huntingdon into a $1.5-billion group employing nearly 6000 people. The Caparo group is now a collection of over 40 companies operating on some 60 locations in the UK, India, Spain, North America, Canada and Dubai. With business interests mainly in the manufacture of steel, automotive and general engineering products, the group's wider activities encompass materials testing, film distribution, hotels and bespoke furniture. And Caparo is still growing. In 2006 alone the group acquired 22 subsidiary companies.

A cohesive family unit is one of the foundations for the success of Paul's empire building. His is no 'rags to riches' story, having had the success of the Apeejay Group behind him when he ventured into the UK. His success is due to a potent mix of hard work, insight, integrity and luck, in varying proportions. 'Whenever and wherever you are an ethnic minority, you always have to put in 120 percent to make it to a 100 percent. My earlier experiences – both as a student and visitor – with the industrialized Western world prepared me for it. If you want to be recognized you have to work harder to prove to everyone that you are one step ahead of them. You have to work harder and with more integrity and honesty.'

On February 18, 1996 Paul stepped down as CEO at Caparo but remained as Chairman. He handed the day-to-day management to his three sons Ambar, Akash and Angad. He was raised to the peerage as Baron Paul of Marylebone in October 1996. He now concentrates on his charity work and improving standards in education. He strongly believes in the unity of the family and in giving the younger generation the best possible education: 'Financial resources can be dissipated; education cannot be lost.'

Paul's three sons, Ambar, Akash and Angad, are responsible for the day-to-day running of the group. With Angad at the helm as Chief Executive it can only get stronger. According to CEO Angad Paul, 'Our strong foundations of family ownership give us the opportunity to take the longer-term view and invest in new companies, products and directions, all of which provide Caparo with the momentum to move forward and continue to grow and succeed.'

Angad – Succession and the New Generation

Angad Paul was born in London and, like his father, attended MIT in Massachusetts, where he received BAs in Economics and Media Arts and Sciences. He became extremely interested in film and pursued this passion immediately upon completing his studies.

Still in his thirties, Angad is a successful movie mogul and has earned a name in the film industry. He helped develop and was a partner in the film *Bombay Boys* which went on to become one of the biggest grossing English films in India. He followed this up by serving as Executive Producer on the Guy Richie film *Lock, Stock and Two Smoking Barrels*, which became a landmark event in British cinema and reached number one at the box office. Paul also served as Executive Producer on the follow-up, *Snatch*, which was released worldwide by Sony Pictures.

He is also a co-owner of both an exclusive London club, Chinawhite, and more recently the Aura Restaurant and bar concept. His daytime job, though, is as the chief executive of the Caparo Group of companies. He is also the Chairman of Established & Sons, a UK-branded furniture design and manufacturing company. In addition, he is a patron of the SHINE Education Trust and the youngest trustee of Slough Grammar School.

His wedding made the headlines, too, when he married Michelle Bonn, a media lawyer, at a ceremony at London Zoo in October 2004. The wedding, which was attended by family members and close friends, was performed in both Hindu and Jewish traditions. Invitation cards bore the Paul crest, with its motto of 'Truth, Freedom and Compassion'. A conservatory was put up in the grounds around the statue of Ambika. 'We decided to celebrate the wedding near Ambika's statue so that we have her presence on such a great family occasion,' said Lord Paul. 'It means a lot to us.'

Racing Cars

There are sure signs that the younger generation, headed by Angad, are making their mark. Caparo has launched the Caparo T1 – one of the star attractions at the world famous UK event, the Goodwood

Festival of Speed. The Caparo T1 is a high-performance two-seater car designed to give customers an affordable and reliable season on the track without incurring the extraordinary costs of running a real Formula One car. These hand-built cars are highly exclusive with a price tag of £180,000. Why racing cars? In true entrepreneurial style, the Pauls set out to convince the large car manufacturers of the benefits of using composites to reduce environmental damage.

Caparo are big players in auto components in the UK, US and India, and they are ever conscious of environmental issues. Much work has been done on reducing fuel consumption to reduce the impact on the environment. The only way they could do this was to reduce the weight of the components. So they went from using steel to using lighter aluminium and then to using composites. They have used composites for their cars, aerospace parts and even boats. No half measures for the Pauls; they hired the entire Formula One team from McLaren who had done a lot of work on composites: 'We hired them all and authorised them to make a racing car from composites.' This was a stroke of genius. The main barriers they faced were from the car manufacturers who had reservations about composites. Now they had proved that they were fast and fashionable; it was a convincing argument and very persuasive. According to Angad, 'It may take 15 to 20 years before we see the widespread use of advanced plastics and composites as an alternative to aluminium and steel in the car industry; nonetheless, we have embarked on this course having recognized that vehicle light-weighting technologies provide Caparo with an excellent commercial opportunity to help car makers reduce vehicle carbon emissions.'

Looking Ahead

When asked about the future Paul declares, 'Our success in the years to come will continue to depend on the skill of our family and management in reacting to opportunities, whilst continuing with

determination, integrity and the principles that have carried us successfully this far.'

The Caparo Group has been built up through a combination of
acquisitions, the organic growth of established businesses and the
development of 'greenfield' projects. The latter demonstrates its skill
at building technology-based steel product companies from scratch
and penetrating export markets.

Under the leadership of Angad, Caparo continues this successful formula for growth. The grouping of independently managed business
units, mainly operating in metal and related markets, gives both critical mass and a stable platform for growth. A customer-oriented philosophy, striving to provide products, services and solutions of the
highest quality at competitive prices is coupled with a lean and flat
corporate structure ensuring low overheads and rapid decision making.
These key features are at the core of Caparo's success.

The Paul family and Caparo are not limited to the engineering industry. Today, the Group's activities include film, hotels, furniture and, of
course, racing cars. These new innovations have been largely due to
the impact of Angad's leadership. Sticking with its now famous strategy of acquisition and innovation but always open to new developments and ideas, and staying true to the 'strong foundations of family
ownership' as well as 'continuing with determination and integrity',
Caparo looks into the future proudly and confidently, aspiring always
for nothing less than excellence.

Accolades

Lord Paul has achieved so much. Honours and awards are too numerous to mention but he has played a key role in the social and educational fields. He was appointed Chancellor of Thames Valley University
and is the first Chancellor of the University of Westminster. He is also
the Chancellor of the University of Wolverhampton. He has had

15 honorary degrees bestowed upon him to date, and has addressed many students worldwide.

He is an Ambassador for British Business. He is also a member of the House of Lords Select Committee on Economic Affairs, and the House of Lords Select Committee on Science & Technology. In 2000, he was appointed to the board of the London Development Agency. He was on the board for the London 2012 Olympics Bid and is now Chairman of the Olympic Delivery Committee, as well as a member of the British Olympic Association Advisory Board.

In a life full of so much tragedy and success, so many experiences both personal and professional, so many highs and lows, Paul recalls two really special and cherished memories. Firstly, when he decided to support former Indian Prime Minister Indira Gandhi in 1977, after she lost the election. His admiration and warmth for her are touching. Secondly, when he was able to hand over the business management of Caparo to his three sons: 'seeing Angad building the company into a high-values engineering business and making the name Caparo into a prestigious brand is a wonderful thing'.

Paul remains actively involved as Chairman of the company and is busier in semi-retirement than ever before. Always one to dabble at the ringside of politics, he claims to enjoy being around politics and politicians but is not interested in political office. 'My expertise lies in different fields and I can serve as much as any politician can from the outside, ' he says. That is why he thrives as Lord Paul of Marylebone. 'You can express your opinions and they count,' he says. Passionate about manufacturing and frustrated at the lack of interest from political parties, he still believes it is the soul and strength of any country. He is philosophical, however. 'Manufacturing is a smaller proportion of the GDP in this country so the emphasis is elsewhere. It's still cheaper to import.'

He has been married to Aruna for over 50 years and he grins even now when he recalls how they met at that fateful party she attended with her fiancé at the time. It has been a long, fulfilling and sustaining relationship and has given him the stability he needed and the family strength and unity which he values so dearly. Like his mother before him, his boys are his jewels, as are his grandchildren.

From a journey that has taken him from the depths of despair and to the highest of joys, he has learnt some very powerful lessons. From his father he learnt 'the dignity of hard work'; from MIT, 'always aspire for the best'; from Mrs Gandhi, 'never lose hope in adverse circumstances'. And, finally, from himself, 'hard work and integrity have no equal'. For Lord Paul, wealth and the trappings of tycoonery are unimportant. 'I have never considered it belongs to me. I am its trustee and must use it to create more wealth. I believe that you must have respect for money and should not go about wasting it and showing off,' he says.

Paul has a warm sense of humour and a mischievous side to him. He still thrives on his work: 'most people get bored with their work and go home. I get bored at home and go to work.' His ambition is undaunted, the flame of desire still burns strong and his rebellious streak is clear to see. In the words of Lord Paul himself, 'Caparo is more than a successful business enterprise – it is a story of people, of values and of human effort. Above all, it is a story of faith and family. I have always believed that hard work and integrity far outweigh any short cuts to success.'

Background Reading

Chhotu, K., *The Swraj Paul Affair*, Slatecount, 1984.
Bisht Mitu, 'Being Swraj Paul' *NRI Achievers, Delhi.* July–Sept. 2007.
Wheatcroft, P., 'Man of Steel with a Touch of Humility', *Daily Telegraph*, April 16, 1994.

Professor Nathu (Nat) Ram Puri

Photo supplied by Professor Nathu Puri

Professor Nathu Puri has managed to combine excellence in professionalism with outstanding business acumen. He is a tall, distinguished man who has experienced highs and lows in life, and who has displayed true grit and resilience in the face of adversity. Often cited as the richest man in Nottingham, where he was better known as the dynamo behind the Melton Medes group, Puri personifies the Asian go-getting spirit. Noted as one of the Asian community's most generous philanthropists, he works hard to give back to a community he cherishes. He has always excelled in his field and has worked tirelessly to build the foundations of his global business Purico – and is worth an estimated £130 million.

Chapter 10

An Early Brush with Politics

Born in 1939 in a small village called Mullan Pur near Chandigarh, India, young Puri had no idea he would one day become one of the most successful Asian entrepreneurs in the UK. He was not from a wealthy background but his family, like most Asian families, prized education for their children, two boys and a girl. Puri needed to fulfil his academic potential so he, like his brother before him, studied for a BA in Pure and Applied Mathematics from the Punjab University, Chandigarh, graduating in 1959. He continued his education and studied Law and Psychology at the same university the following year but had to leave midway due to pressing family needs. He had to go home to manage a small truck for the family, who could not afford to hire someone else to do it. It appears that whilst he was at University he got involved in politics, went on to fight elections and was '...involved with some behaviour I'm not so proud of', he admits.

When contemplating his future he realized, 'It's bad to be a politician in India as it's no career, you're either at the top or the bottom.' He explains further: 'Most politicians in India tended to be people who have failed in other things or came from rich families – it's a precarious career.' There was no future in this. 'I had nothing to fall back on'.

Puri decided that the UK was the most sensible place to obtain professional qualifications. He enrolled as a student at National College,

Borough Polytechnic (now London South Bank University) in London, for a one-year diploma course in air conditioning and refrigeration. 'This was all my family could afford. This was not my course of choice but it was the only one available we could afford,' he recalls. More importantly it was approved for release of foreign exchange by the Reserve Bank of India. At that time the maximum foreign currency you could otherwise take out of the country was £3 and this was not a viable amount to study with. Puri gained his Diploma in Refrigeration and Air Conditioning in 1967. After finishing his studies, he started his career in the UK with F G Skerritt Limited, a Nottingham-based engineering company, to gain some experience before going back to India. It would prove to be a propitious step. The next 18 months saw Puri working over 80 hours a week. He was on a steep learning curve with the job, and was also doing private work in addition to gain practical experience of installations as well as to earn and save some money.

His student visa had expired and extensions were to come to an end in October 1969, but he decided to return early to India in March. He had saved a fair amount of money for a reasonable start back home. Using his new-found knowledge, he got a job with a refrigeration company in Bombay, but it did not work out. He found it difficult to settle there. 'I was not credible,' he says. By that he means that people thought he had obtained the job through connections rather than merit – 'It's because he knows so and so', is what the relatives thought. 'Maybe they thought I was the same person they knew 21 years ago, with no experience or qualifications.' He reasons, 'None of these comments were made with malice, rather in a matter of fact way and may be even with a sense of pride. But I had worked very hard to learn and succeed in a foreign place and such comments, after a time, hurt.' Furthermore, he recalls, 'it did not help me to settle down as Bombay was so far away from Punjab'. Puri is, above all else, a proud man determined to stand on his own two feet. He didn't want to feel he 'did not merit his position'. India is very competitive and people are quick to judge. The close-knit family and community is a way of life with Asian families but it can be both helpful and stifling.

Strong Foundations

Puri's fortunes were about to change, and within three months he was in demand. 'The Nottingham company asked me to come back; they valued my work ethic. I was offered 50 percent more salary compared to what I'd been getting paid three months earlier and a company car.' F G Skerritt wanted him to head up the design team and use his expertise to help them win the bid for two major European projects. He rejoined after Skerritt obtained a work permit for him. From 1967 he progressed from intermediate engineer to project engineer, to senior engineer, to section leader and to manager. He left Skerritt in July 1975, but was to go back in January 1983 to acquire the company.

Skerritt was not awarded the two major European projects in the end, but Puri worked on a series of other lucrative ones. There were 10 engineers in the company and he, together with his team of two assistants, generated more than 50 percent of company profits. He also obtained all his work through competitive tendering whereas others mostly dealt with negotiated work. He worked tirelessly, refusing to be paid overtime but instead agreeing on a percentage of the profit from each project. He was prepared to put in as much time as it took to complete each project above a certain level. This innovative approach meant that he was eventually the highest-earning employee in the company after the chief executive.

Hard work is the backbone of Puri's success, but his drive was to gain knowledge: 'I wanted to learn as much as I could; it was important.' He had left India for a reason and needed to prove himself, and so a simple nine-to-five routine was not sufficient to achieve his goals. He was determined to succeed. He was also conscious that he lacked the practical grounding required: 'I had the theory, but I did not have the necessary background experience; I had not served the normal apprenticeship.' He had to work '...extra hard to learn the trade and not to look a fool with the operatives who worked on my projects'. This is one of the essential ingredients of Asian entrepreneurial success in the UK. The first generation of Asians left a lot behind to come here, both emotionally and psychologically. There was enormous sacrifice despite the lure of greater opportunities. It's not enough just to make do and survive. You feel you have to make it, somehow or other. This is a key driver.

His hard work paid off: 'my disadvantage became an advantage'. He had no prior knowledge and so could learn from scratch and by analysis. There were no bad habits to be undone and he could be shaped accordingly. Ignorance is bliss, sometimes. In 1975 he left the company on a matter of principle but he had gained a reputation for his innovative approach to solving problems, meeting deadlines and trimming costs, which were key drivers for success in an industry used to working at a leisurely pace.

Puri initially set up as a contractor and soon became a consultant, working mainly on hospitals installations and design. Puri's own company, Environment Design Consultants, was set up in January 1976 and he became the sole partner soon after. This was a building, design and consultancy practice and continued to be semi-active until 1983. In late 1975, the Royal National Orthopaedic Hospital wanted air conditioning installed for their operating theatres before the next summer so they approached him. They had a limited budget and a six-month time frame for completion. Everyone who had been approached previously said that they needed double the money and would have to close the theatres for three months – this was an unacceptable option for the hospital, already under pressure to perform more efficiently. Puri was recommended by someone who had dealt with him at F G Skerritt and knew of his innovative approach to problem solving. Puri took up the challenge in January 1976, setting up his consultancy practice. He managed to do the job with the theatres closed for only two days, plus a Bank Holiday weekend. 'I am a practical person. I am not afraid of hard work and I think with the customer in mind, ' he says. He realised how crucial it was to have the theatres working so he minimized the time they had to be closed. 'We wanted to do every job, no matter how large or small, to the best of our ability and I used all my contacts in the industry, calling on many favours,' he asserts proudly. 'At that time I did not even know what to charge for the services we provided; I wanted to meet my commitment and we did. I was soon in great demand at many post-graduate teaching hospitals. I soon learnt to charge "proper" rates for the job. Operating theatre project fees barely covered the costs.'

Another example of his innovative approach demonstrates why he has become one of UK's most respected entrepreneurs. This time, it was to do with coal-fired boiler houses at many RAF stations, which were mainly pre-World War Two in date. These boiler houses were of immense importance and so, when other engineers said they would have to be shut for many weeks to complete the job, incredibly Puri would shut them for only one afternoon and the job would still be completed to the same specification. 'Of course, we got paid much more for the service,' he professes proudly. He professes proudly. He knew his value and also the immense amount of time and money he saved others. 'Think of the cost of alternatives for the customers. I soon learnt to charge premier rates for our services.'

The Birth of Melton Medes

Having achieved a tremendous amount of success with his own consultancy, he sought further growth. It was then that he made the bold move to buy F G Skerritt Ltd, the very company he had originally worked for. He was uncertain if it was for sale but had heard rumours through the grapevine. He asked his accountant to sound out the company. 'I did not want to disclose my interests as I thought it may embarrass the incumbent management and the owners who I knew personally,' he says with typical Asian restraint. He finally did reveal himself and a deal was made. Digby Jones was one of the solicitors (at Edge and Ellison) who advised the vendors,

He realized, with the acquisition of F G Skerritt Ltd, that 'it's easier and quicker to buy companies than build them up from scratch.' His formula was to find specialist under-performing companies in a bad state and turn them around. After the acquisition of a small manufacturing company in January 1984, he found manufacturing easier to deal with than construction. 'I fell in love with manufacturing and mainly bought struggling manufacturing companies thereafter,' he reminisces. This meant he could buy at very competitive rates, add tremendous value to the companies and increase their turnover, reducing costs and start making profits.

He called his organization Melton Medes. It was founded in January 1983 when acquiring F G Skerritt Ltd and F G Skerritt (Contracts) Ltd. Since then, the Melton Medes Group has achieved phenomenal growth with over 20 acquisitions in the UK and United States, and it became a substantial industrial holding company. Interests include plastics, processing, paper and packaging, carpets and fabrics, and engineering.

So how did he get the money to buy F G Skerritt? 'I was fighting a court case with the Department of Health for unpaid fees,' he explains. 'I settled at the steps of the court for £670,000 plus costs and used that money to buy the company.' Puri continues, 'It was just as well,' he recalls. 'I was struggling, I had to borrow from the bank to fight the case – the manager was supportive but was limited to only a certain amount.' Puri found that banks were conservative. 'Later I was trusted enough to have substantial unsecured loans.' However, it is the early stages, when you are unproven that you need the most help, and 'not knowing how to prepare a proper business plan did not help in the new banking climate'. The banks had switched to a more formula-based approach, rather than the personal touch, judging each case on its merit.

Puri grew in confidence and exercised his business acumen as well as his professional skills while making acquisitions. He was cautious and says, 'I did well by buying my businesses slowly'. His caution dates back to growing up in a modest household: 'If you don't have a rich family, you need to be more innovative. Steps need to be taken one after the other and not at a fast pace because of the lack of resources, especially early on.' His approach to the subsequent acquisitions was both entrepreneurial and innovative – and typically Asian. 'I didn't borrow to buy, but got the maximum out of the existing company and used it to finance the next one. Later on, after making the changes, say over two or three months, I used assets and collateral to the full to arrange new facilities which I would use for the next acquisition.' This method was not without its limitations: 'Of course it restricted the size of the next deal we did'. The businesses he bought were loss makers and Puri was turning them around, so 'soon the banks became more confident about our ability as we grew'.

In 1992, between the UK and US, 'I had borrowed £90 million and had another £30 million available as undrawn and no one had even heard of me! But no one said "no" because of our success. I was even given a £10 million unsecured loan by one bank and £5 million by another for acquisitions! These were large sums in the 1980s.' He continues, 'Once you are seen as a successful businessman everyone wants to join the party.'

So what drives Puri? 'When you buy a business, you want to ensure you are successful and that you did not make a mistake. This is what drives me.' How does this dynamo celebrate his success? 'I won't say I get a buzz out of it exactly but every once in a while I have a smile and glass of whisky to toast that it was not a bad decision and it turned out OK.' He adds, 'This is maybe after a year or 18 months once the company has proved successful.' He feels strongly that success is about inner self-satisfaction, not to show others. 'We do not have a 100 percent record but in the first 10 years we made over 25 acquisitions in manufacturing and no failures.' In later years, when he started spending more and more time overseas, the success rate fell.

When asked to explain the basis of his success, he explains that good decision making is vital. 'I was lucky with finding a Chief Executive early on and some of the management people we inherited with the companies took to new ways of managing the business well.' He explains, 'Communication lines became very short for decision making, and 99 percent of the key decisions were made within the companies where the new chairman, if convinced, would authorise them.' Puri continues to expand on his successful formula. 'I did not chair any of the subsidiary companies and only sat in three board meetings of our private companies during all the years. I normally resigned my directorships of new companies within days of acquiring control. I stay focused on my part of the job.' With the organization growing so well, he says, 'we created rules but gave freedom to operate within those rules. These were verbally explained to the persons acting as Chairmen of companies, there was nothing written down. It worked 99 percent of the time'. When it comes to making decisions, he cautions, 'It's important not to make a decision too early and never until you have to make it. If you are too early, you make it based on just the information you have to hand and start discounting when contrary further information comes along'. Once he has made a decision, Puri asserts, 'then I am clear and I stay focused as no other alternative exists'.

Despite all the good intentions, international success and growth, he was to face a major challenge.

The Demise of Melton Medes

He was met with an unfortunate problem emanating from the workplace. 'When you are successful there are always problems. You learn to deal with these routinely.' He had problems with one of the trade unions. 'The issue had arisen in the aftermath of Maxwell's controversial death/suicide. The same trade union which was at Maxwell plants hyped the situation to divert attention from their failure there, and then others joined in who were equally negligent.' He recalls the situation which gave him much anguish.

Perhaps Puri was in the wrong place at the wrong time? There had been several high-profile cases in the headlines at the time such as the Polly Peck and Maxwell scandals. The BCCI scandal was also uppermost in people's minds; this had hit the Asian community particularly badly. Puri feels he was the victim in the aftermath of the Maxwell pensions fiasco and other similar cases. This cast a shadow over the whole private pensions industry.

'There was no comparison, our pension funds were in surplus but it did not stop detractors,' Puri says. He asserts, 'You must always defend yourself and your integrity. Maybe after their failure to deal with Maxwell, they needed to show they were still on the job.'

In the 1990s Puri was accused of questionable legal practices by allegedly raiding a company pension fund in the UK. The Graphical, Printing and Media Union (GPMU), based in England, charged Puri with arranging a low-interest loan from a company pension fund to enterprises held by Puri's Melton Medes Group. The loans were repaid not in cash but in shares of a public company. Following the transfer, within six months, shares in the company plummeted. He had also invested money in property which was again questioned.

Puri is quick to defend himself. 'Our reputation was on the line. We had to fight to defend it. Our pension funds were in surplus. I understood the cost of drawn-out litigation both in cash and opportunity cost, but not to defend ourselves in the charged atmosphere of the time would have given our business a bad name.' He continues, 'In 1992 John Smith, then shadow chancellor in the Labour Party, rang me up to ask if I would agree to put my name to supporting his alternative budget. I told him it might not be a good idea as my name was under attack in the press, and he said "oh, the article in the *FT*", and I said "yes". He said, "I know, and we are satisfied it is journalistic licence , we have checked". I said "if you have no problem then go ahead and add my name, I am happy to support you".'

One of the accusations against him was that he sold one of the subsidiary company properties to the pension scheme for too little, 'Reality was not relevant,' he explains ruefully. 'When an elephant is walking, a lot of insects live off it.' His experience has shown him that if you are respected and known, then certain people will try to disparage you and pull you down. 'There is an element of jealousy from some quarters and, if it is affecting the morale of the firm and causing problems, then you have to fight these people.' This was not easy but Puri has a fighting spirit. Not fighting was not an option. 'I have lost more money than people ever thought I had in the first place,' he confesses. At the height of the court case he also found himself with family issues requiring urgent attention. He had one brother and a sister. In March, 1995 his elder brother had a stroke while flying back from Singapore and lost his speech and was bedridden for quite some time. His sister, a widow, was found to have a malignant brain tumour a few weeks later in April, 1995 and passed away few months later. He ended up compromising and settling the case.

Bruised by the experience but not downcast or bitter, Puri is philosophical and detached. 'You can't be emotional and be a good businessman. It was a long time ago and we still managed to flourish. When you encounter prejudice, it stems from ignorance and jealousy but it is very damaging.' He fought long and hard and costs amounted to around £40 million, but 'I survived', he says proudly, 'and I have gone on to do better'. He is resilient. The insults served to make him stronger. He put in greater effort and become even more successful: 'I will always do my best in whatever I am involved in.'

He recalls his early years where he did not encounter racism from management working in F G Skerritt Ltd, or even from other senior people later on. 'Once I was in the company, the effort I made and the results I achieved were more important than the colour of my skin or the country I came from.' Regardless, it was a sad state of affairs. After this expensive fiasco and troubles with Melton Medes he decided to move some of the companies out from under the Melton Medes umbrella. This spelled the demise of Melton Medes, but the start of a new era with Purico.

How to Make and Lose a Fortune – Perspectives from Nat Puri

'Success is accidental', says a philosophical Puri, 'it cannot always be planned.' He made a lot of money and lost a lot, and accepts there is no rhyme or reason or set formula: 'Luck plays a role in business and in life. You can benefit enormously from a situation or a string of events. Of course you need to put in the effort.' Behind this belief in fatalism is the reality that Puri worked very hard for his success. It was effort and expertise that got him the recognition that was to set him apart from others.

The best strategy, according to Puri, is to work hard and to do the right thing. 'Integrity is important,' he says. 'You have to ultimately live with yourself and have to do things according to your values. Don't take abuse lying down.' Puri emphasises the importance of the work ethic. 'Even if you work for other people put your heart and soul into it. Work hard no matter what the situation and who it is for, rewards will come. Commit yourself to your goals. If you have made a decision, see it through. Without my hard work at Skerritts and what I learnt during that period I would never have achieved the level of success I did later in life.'

A New Era – the Purico Group of Companies

Puri now operates the Purico Group of Companies, which includes F G Skerritt Ltd. His reach is global with a strong presence in China and the US. The Group's interests are diversified: 'I haven't even seen all my businesses. We had a company in Malaysia, it is sold now. I never went to see it!'

Puri enjoyed success in the US where he first bought a 90 percent share in a couple of hospitals in October 1988. Although he never saw them, he sold them a few years later at a reasonable profit. With the proceeds, Puri bought into a printing company, acquiring a 51 percent share for £1 million. This was a good move as he managed to increase his equity stake without investing more in the business. He also got £22.5 million in cash dividends and in 1999 he sold the business for $201 million, netting an additional $60 million. 'Luck plays a big role,' he says philosophically.

His skill is in turning things around. F G Skerritt Ltd was a loss maker when he took it over, but now turnover has multiplied by over 1000 percent to over £40 million a year. It has regularly made profits of over £1 million in the last three to four years. Puri's strength is that he is an entrepreneur and a qualified professional at the top of his profession, a rare combination. 'Normally engineers work for others but numbers are my strength. I studied pure and applied mathematics. In my family it doesn't matter if you understand anything else or not, you must understand numbers. So my love of maths helps me to grasp figures very quickly and that gives me my entrepreneurial edge,' he says.

Giving Back to the Community

A devoted family man, Puri is married to Davi, a Danish lady, and has one son. He says, 'I used to work night and day; I took on too many jobs. I was always chasing money and saving it.' He recalls, 'It was important to me at the time, as I was not from a well-off family.' This all changed for him one day in February 1969. 'Before deciding to go back to India I was just thinking about my life in UK, it suddenly dawned on me that money must be a means to provide and not an end in itself, and since then my emphasis has been different.' His realization was further impacted two years later when his father died, 'for the *barah* [paying respects], some 1500 people came for the last meal. It was a very emotional occasion as many people he had helped during his life cried. It made me feel very humble. I believed then and do even today that whatever I achieve, I will never achieve the love and respect he enjoyed. He helped others when he did not have much money. Compared to him all my contributions are insignificant.'

Over and above what he does for the community, he is very proud of his heritage and promotes it. 'I am Indian and a representative of the Indian community; I want the things I do to reflect well on other Indians.' Even his latest award, an Honorary Doctorate from South Bank University awarded in November 2007, and a recognition from Chandighar University cannot stop this man from pressing ahead with his portfolio of social and business engagements. He is now retired, but in true Asian style has kept it in the family. His nephew Anil Puri is the Chair of the Group and several of his executives have grown and developed within the company.

It is not only as a successful businessman that Nat Puri is celebrated; he is also famed for his philanthropic contributions and love of sports. He set up the Puri Foundation in June 1988 and all the funds within it have been donated by Puri or his companies. The focus of the Puri Foundation has been the relief of poverty, community projects and research. He recently set up an educational trust and they have developed 500 schools in Nepal and intend to raise enough money to set up 10,000 more schools in South Asia. According to his wife Davi, 'Nat is a very generous person'. His love for cricket has taken him around the world and many cricketers are amongst his closest friends. Farokh Engineer, an Indian cricket legend and long term friend says of him, 'Nat is a tremendous credit to our Indian community. People like me, Sunil Gavaskar and Kapil Dev are all privileged to have him as our good friend. I've always called him more famous than Robin Hood in Nottingham!' Another example of his spontaneous, playful side is illustrated when he gave Virendar Sehwag £50,000 for being the first Indian cricketer to score 300 runs in a test match inning!

Perween Warsi

Photo supplied by Perween Warsi

The unstoppable Perween Warsi is the dynamic woman behind the Derby-based S&A Foods, named after her sons Sadiq and Abid. Perween was born and brought up in Bihar in northern India and was in the kitchen helping to prepare special dishes for family occasions from the age of 4. She later married Talib, a doctor, and moved to the UK, finally settling in Derby. Increasingly dissatisfied with the quality of Indian products already on the market, Perween decided to take the plunge and started her own business using her family recipes. She was soon in great demand and made a major breakthrough when she won a contract, in a blind tasting competition, to supply the major supermarket chain Asda. The rest, as they say, is history. Since then, the business has enjoyed a meteoric rise and now employs several hundred people. For many this would be a familiar tale. It shows the importance of family as both the roots and branches of success, it deals with turning a passion into a wealth-generating business and, like so many others, it is about adaptation to a new environment. Perween Warsi is no 'silent contributor', quiet and unassuming behind the scenes. She is one of the best known Asian businesswomen in the UK and is worth an estimated £70 million.

Chapter 11

Roots of Success

Though she was born and brought up in the province of Bihar, Perween Warsi's father was an engineer and his work meant that the family constantly moved around the country. This early exposure to a nomadic lifestyle gave Perween a great capacity to adapt, something she would later need. She grew up in a large family of three brothers and one sister, fairly comfortably off with servants to hand. As a small child, a playful Perween would continually harass the servants until they gave in and let her help prepare the meals. She undertook little tasks such as folding the samosas and kneading chapatti dough. Although Perween did not grow up in an entrepreneurial family, she credits her family for her inspiration and for enabling her passion for food to flourish. From an early age she watched her mother and grandmother create recipes from a variety of fresh ingredients.

Food plays a pivotal role in Indian culture, where dinner parties and functions are centred around lavish banquets. The smells, flavours and colours of the herbs and spices are scintillating and tease the senses. Families sit down and eat together and no guest is allowed to leave a household without being offered refreshments. The various regions have their own specialties. For example, rice and coconut are associated with southern areas and dishes such as masala dosas are popular in south India, while chappatis, tandoor dishes and lentils are fashionable in the north.

Perween's Indian heritage and early experiences have played a signifi-
cant role in her entrepreneurial approach to business. The constant
movement from place to place meant that the young Perween enjoyed
the varied cultures and flavours of different parts of India, without any
restraints. She grew up to respect the traditions and to understand her
cultural heritage and yet was prepared to break the mould if need be.
Change has always been part of the entrepreneur equation, whether it
is the entrepreneur seeing the change before it happens, changing
faster than anyone else or accepting change as a key part of life. For
Perween change has become normal, something she embraces from
her childhood and upbringing, and something that now forms one of
the key building blocks of her business.

Her passion for food developed alongside her entrepreneurial skills
and visions. Alert to the environment around her and with a constant
need to improve quality, she dreamt of running a school as early as her
teens. She spent hours planning her ideal school, trying to improve on
her existing experiences. The school was not to be. Her life took a new
turn when at the age of 17 Perween married Talib Warsi, a doctor, in
a traditional arranged match. In 1975 they migrated to Britain, living
first in Wales and then in Yorkshire before finally settling in Derby in
the house in which they still live. England was a complete culture
shock for her, not just because she had to adjust to the cold climate
but also because she no longer had the comfort of servants. She was
now faced with the task of cooking and cleaning and looking after her
husband while Talib worked as a general practitioner in Derby.

Rebel with a Cause

Britain has a long-standing past with India and Britain has embraced
Indian food as if it were its own invention. From the early days of Brits
enjoying a few beers and a curry to the more sophisticated, wider
range of dishes that are now well known, Indian food is a huge industry. There are an estimated 8000 Indian restaurants in Britain and it

seems that Chicken Tikka Masala is now more popular than fish and chips. Hard to believe, really!

Perween's starting point came about in a reactionary way: 'I wanted to challenge the food industry. I found supermarket food to be boring, tasteless and poor value for money.' Her mission was to provide better tasting food. 'I am passionate about this,' she affirms. In 1986, with the support of her family and friends, Perween decided to create a business using her own recipes. She had been increasingly dissatisfied with the quality of Indian products already on the market. She started off a tiny cottage industry which was later to grow into a major enterprise – S&A Foods. Her first step was to produce finger-food in her own kitchen for a local Greek restaurant. She was soon in great demand, began to market herself more effectively and the orders poured in.

Perween extended her kitchen and began to employ a number of women. Most of these women were fellow Asians and many of them did not speak English fluently. She has watched them develop over the years, together with her business, and many of them are now able to operate very complex machinery and have gained tremendously in both confidence and fluency of the English language. Perween nurtured talent and gave opportunities to these women in the early days. In return, she has been rewarded with a loyal, stable staff base, many of whom have been with her from the start.

Soaring to New Heights

So what does it take to make a success of business in this, one of the most competitive of industries? First you overcome the hurdles and barriers which come from any number of sources: family commitments, experience, lack of finance. Then you don't give up. You never give up. Perween had always set her sights on greater things. For her, the key ingredients to success are persistence and determination. She never shied away from rejection and had so much faith in the quality of her products that she continued to contact supermarkets to convince them to trial her products.

Look at most entrepreneurs who have been successful and you will see some kind of chronological serendipity combined with a geographic disposition. Some find themselves in the right place at the right time but are the only ones to notice. Others deliberately move in the opposite direction to everyone else and create that time and place themselves. Inevitably there will be luck involved but luck is something anyone can have. The judgment is in knowing the time and the place is right and being able to do something about it.

Although luck played a part in Perween's success, it was no accident that Asda was her big break. She had hounded the supermarkets so it was just a matter of time before the doors opened. Perween was invited by Asda to participate in a blind tasting event; her food would sit alongside other samples. This was to be her making. It was a major breakthrough; her products proved popular and her dream of hitting the big time came a step closer.

It was in 1987 that she won her first major contract to supply chilled and frozen dishes to the supermarket. This success, however, was not without its challenges for as S&A Foods became increasingly successful Perween realized that larger premises were needed to accommodate the growing business. She needed to expand rapidly in order to meet the orders and access to finance was proving to be difficult. Financiers were cautious and were looking for at least a three-year track record. Her few months of experience in her own kitchen did not leave them feeling comfortable about the venture.

Perween recalls, 'We had our savings and what little we could borrow but it was nowhere near enough to build a factory.' After some deliberation she joined forces with the Hughes Food Group, a local company, in order to generate the funds necessary to build a factory. 'We were not strong enough financially to build a factory on our own,' she explains, and so she sold some shares to the Hughes Food Group. A purpose-built factory was designed specifically to produce chilled Indian ready meals and by 1989 the first S&A Foods factory was built in Derby, creating over 100 jobs in the area. Further contracts to supply Asda and Safeway were signed and S&A Foods grew, and established itself in an industrial unit in Shaftsbury Street South in Derby. The success of S&A Foods enabled Talib to quit his profession and join her full time. He has now retired from managing the marketing of the company.

Losing Control?

Success continued and the business flourished. Always with her ear to the ground and staying abreast of the latest trends, Perween soon caught on to the new Balti craze which was sweeping Birmingham. She was creative, introducing a greater variety of dishes, and innovating with packaging. However, she was soon to face a new challenge.

Like many other businesses S&A Foods faced the recession head-on. But then, in 1990–91, they were dealt a devastating blow. Despite their own business performing well, the parent company was in trouble. Within a few years of them joining the Hughes Food Group it faced financial difficulty and went into receivership. This meant that Perween's portion of shares also went into receivership. They were worth only about £4 million then and so she could easily have given up and sold out. She shudders in horror even today at the thought of losing it all. 'We were devastated, all our work was in the company and all my efforts and that of those around me. I had little choice but to show potential buyers around our premises but it hurt me.' She continues, 'I was in despair. I did not know what was going to happen in the future and yet the day-to-day business was very real. We still had to carry on producing our meals. We had to develop new products, recruit staff and continue knowing there may not be a tomorrow for us. But', she states firmly, 'I could not give in.'

This was a grim time and it took all Perween's resolve, grit and determination to get through it. 'We were not prepared to give up. We

believed in our products and in ourselves. We had a good relationship
with our customers and suppliers and our employees. We fought the
case and won,' she says of the fraught battle after Hughes went into
receivership. 'I didn't sell, I refused to give in and we went independent.' She recalls, 'They were harrowing months when we were being
hounded by people trying to buy us.' The Warsi family fought to regain
control and, after a long-drawn battle, Perween and her husband completed a management buy-out in November 1991 with the backing of
the venture capitalists, 3i. Perween later bought back the shares and in
May 2004 regained 100 percent ownership of the company.

Recalling that period Perween says, 'I have dealt with a lot of challenges over the years but have not once been even close to giving up.'
It's difficult to imagine this woman closing the shop door. Perween
certainly has not had it easy. This was a very difficult period not only
because of the legal troubles; the company also faced stiff competition.
Many food manufacturers were competing for a share of the lucrative
ready-meal business and Perween had to find ways to remain ahead of
the game. Not one to compromise on quality, she is very hands-on and
involved with product development: 'I insist on the highest standards
and quality.' They have expanded their range of products beyond
Indian ready meals and now include Oriental and American foods. 'I
have excellent chefs working on recipes,' Perween says.

Growth of an Empire

In 1996, with S&A Foods' continuing success and need for expansion,
an £8 million bespoke factory was built next to the original site. Since
then the business has continued to prosper so that it now employs
over 600 people. This has enabled S&A Foods to strengthen its position in the UK and overseas markets and to meet growing demands for
supermarket own-label meals as well as its own range of branded
products. The company has ventured into France, Holland and
Denmark as part of a concerted export initiative.

New product development is vital for the business to sustain its momentum and Perween spends much of her time travelling the world and sampling different dishes with a view to developing future recipes. At the start her vision was national; now it is global. The company head-hunted two chefs from five-star hotels in India to help develop new meals and expand into new cuisines such as Chinese food, which in April 1996 involved the launch of a new range of quality dishes with TV chef Ken Hom.

So, within a decade, Perween has built up an international business employing hundreds of people with a turnover of around £60 million. With the backing and commitment of her staff and family, Perween's entrepreneurial spirit and hard work has resulted in numerous awards for food quality, product innovation and business success. In 1997, when S&A foods celebrated its tenth official anniversary, Perween was awarded an honorary MBA by the University of Derby and appointed to the Department of Trade and Industry Advisory Committee on Competitiveness. In the same year, she received a well-earned MBE in the New Year's Honours list.

Perween Warsi is an example of the very essence of the dynamic entrepreneurial woman and she has exploited the food revolution to overcome barriers that would, and have, deterred many others. She is no stereotypical silent entrepreneur. She has the steely resolve necessary to thrive in the competitive world of mass-market catering. Yet she is still from a background where her family have supported her and continue to play a pivotal role in her business. She herself states that without the support of her husband and family this level of success would not have been possible.

How to Make a Fortune – Perspectives from Perween

As many of these profiles show to the outsider looking in, the most exciting thing about these people is not necessarily the things they have done but rather what we can learn from what they have done.

Perween Warsi has broken the mould; a rapid-growth business in a mature and slow-growing industry, a small player in a sea of giant retailers. Success has been hard fought and well earned. What can we learn? First, you do something you believe in, something you really care about. Second, you treat your people as people. People are assets so take care of them, get them involved. Perween is passionate about innovation and high standards when it comes to food and she encourages everyone in the business to get involved. From the CEO to the shop floor, no one is exempt from the responsibility of coming up with new ideas, be they in design, packaging or processing. In an industry which demands innovation, this is a company where it is expected from everyone. She attempts to instil a family culture within the company and is hands-on, keeping abreast of daily events and being concerned about the welfare of her workers.

There is no right or wrong way to run a business, no theory that fits all. Each business is different and you have to tailor decisions for your business. Having the right mindset is important, she says. 'I employ people who are open minded and open to learning. You must keep on learning. I don't like people with fixed, closed minds who are not prepared to learn.' She avoids egos and closed minds where possible as, 'you can't wake a person who is pretending to be asleep'. She adds, 'To succeed you need common sense, confidence, determination and a positive mindset.'

There have been different challenges in each period of the business. 'It's not a challenge to find people to employ but it is a huge challenge to find the "right" people. You can't teach them how to have a positive mindset.'

The people she employs must fit into the S&A family culture which is innovative and creative but also supportive. Perween values her employees and feels they are best placed to offer advice on their own jobs: 'The people on the factory floor know the challenges of their jobs, they are empowered to help make improvements and increase efficiency. I talk to them, I listen to them.' In fact she has set up fort-nightly listening groups where they discuss how they can improve things, and see if there is a better way of doing things. 'The business is about people and products not bricks and mortar,' she states firmly. 'I am fortunate to be surrounded by excellent people at all levels of my business.' The people she employs provide 600-plus reasons why she has this formula right.

Key Turning Points

Perween's life has certainly not been dull, but from all the highs and lows two events are particularly special: 'The most important and spe-cial part of my life was having my two boys, and now my grand-daughter. The family means everything to me.

'The other moments I cherish are when my products win awards. I am passionate about my products and their quality. We have won awards in innovation, training and development and in 2006 we won the best supermarket ready-food award for our Tikka Masala.' There are many accolades this women has received, and she is proud of them. 'They give me immense pleasure and show that the hard work has been recognised and has paid off,' she says.

One of the keys to her success is determination. Perween has a res-olute spirit in the face of challenge and near disaster. 'To be a good leader', she explains, 'you have to have a winning attitude and be enthusiastic about the business, only then can you enthuse others. You have to keep people motivated and engaged.'

She is passionate about innovation – 'Innovation is vital for the lifeblood of the company' – and lives by the motto 'innovate or die'. Perween is aware of other companies close to her heels and says, 'This is a crowded, cut-throat market with high standards; we have to stay ahead.' In order to do this she empowers everyone from the shop floor upwards to have a say. 'We encourage people to speak their minds. We have a "my bright idea" scheme, where people can put forward their ideas and we have a panel who note any winning ideas.' This positive mindset empowers staff and they feel they are heard and can make important changes.

There are no moans or whines about being a woman or being Asian; both are pluses as far as Perween is concerned. 'I have not experienced negative prejudice in my career as a businesswoman.' She continues, 'I am me, I am who I am. I have confidence in myself. I have knowledge, I have the expertise. My gender is irrelevant.' Her passion for her business and its success, together with her sensitivity in dealing with people and situations, has held her in good stead. Perween has a high level of self-esteem and a lot of inner confidence. 'I love challenges, I thrive on them,' she explains enthusiastically.

And life is not without challenges: 'There are always going to be obstacles in life be it personal or professional. I am not a quitter.' She undeniably has courage, determination and positive thinking in heaps. 'I try and break barriers. There has to be a better way of doing things,' she says, speaking like the true entrepreneur she is.

'Now we have expanded and supply the food service sector and restaurants as well as some of the other major supermarkets,' Perween says. They have also extended their operations into France and Germany: 'I want to create an international brand so that every one can enjoy my quality products. My vision is to have an international presence and we are getting there.'

Her son Sadiq and her husband are in the business alongside her, while her other son Abid has decided to pursue other opportunities, for now at least. Her Indian heritage and its values with respect to family are very important to Perween. She appreciates the importance of support: 'Women generally support their husbands, I was lucky mine supported me. I could not have done this without the support of my husband. He used to help me in the factory even after a long day in the surgery.' They have both worked so hard, particularly in the early days when Perween had two infant sons to look after and Talib was a full-time working doctor in a busy practice. 'The early days were not easy. I was juggling everything. I was in anguish because I was not willing to compromise anything. My family were important and my sons so young they needed their mother and yet I could not give up on the business, it was my passion and I was determined to see it through.' She credits her family, friends and the people around her for seeing her through.

And what is next for this female dynamo? Her vision is for a global brand, and if anyone can get there it is Perween. Her ability to override storms and knock down barriers has meant she has remained for many years the consummate role model. 'Hopefully, one day people worldwide will eat tasty, wholesome food,' she says. Perween is still only in her early fifties and is vivacious, bright and confident. She is an intelligent woman with a lot of common sense and emotional intelligence. She is a woman who has enjoyed the full spectrum of being a mother, a wife, an entrepreneur and a role model. She remains passionate and enthusiastic about food and the business without compromising her family values. They come first. She loves her children and dotes on her grandchild.

In a turbulent world she epitomizes the successful Asian female entrepreneur, of whom little is written but – now – something is known.

Background Reading

Clark, E., 'Perween Warsi: Food is in my blood', BBC News Online Business Reporter, Sept. 19, 2002.

Dhaliwal, S., Silent Contributors – Asian Female Entrepreneurs and Women in Business, Roehampton Institute, 1998.

Afterword

This book, 'Making a Fortune - Learning from the Asian Phenomenon' is about Asian entrepreneurs in Britain. It describes the triumphs and challenges which these individuals faced and how they overcame the obstacles to make a success of their ventures. A common thread running through these incredible stories is their sheer determination and hard work. As Thomas Alva Edison said, *'Genius is one per cent inspiration and ninety-nine per cent perspiration'*. Asian success is talked about a great deal and a number of reasons are advanced as to why British Asians are at the cutting edge. This book illustrates through the stories of these dynamic business people how they have succeeded. It goes behind the superficial assertions and illuminates some of the real factors which have contributed to their progress. These are human stories which will be of interest to a much wider audience and not just academics and budding entrepreneurs. All those featured in this book have grown from small beginnings into major businesses and have aspirations which no doubt will propel them into world wide concerns. As John Harvey-Jones said, *'I think this is an exciting picture of tomorrow's world. I think that business leadership is in itself an honourable, testing, imaginative and creative job. It is not just about creation of wealth, it is about creation of a better world for tomorrow and the building and growing of people.'*

These are unfinished stories, stories of struggle, adventure and achievement from which all of us can seek inspiration. There is more to come. There is a difference between making money and creating wealth for others. These individuals are already on that path. They are now making a much wider contribution to society. This is a timely and an exciting book.

Learn, be inspired, and marvel at the human spirit illustrated in this book.

Usha Prashar
The Baroness Prashar of Runneymede CBE

Index